Robert Peary
and the Quest for the North Pole

WORLD EXPLORERS

Robert Peary
and the Quest for the North Pole

Christopher Dwyer

Introductory Essay by Michael Collins

CHELSEA HOUSE PUBLISHERS

New York · Philadelphia

On the cover   Map of the North Pole; portrait of Robert Peary

Chelsea House Publishers
Editor-in-Chief   Richard S. Papale
Managing Editor   Karyn Gullen Browne
Copy Chief   Philip Koslow
Picture Editor   Adrian G. Allen
Assistant Art Director   Howard Brotman
Series Design   Loraine Machlin
Manufacturing Director   Gerald Levine
Systems Manager   Lindsey Ottman
Production Coordinator   Marie Claire Cebrián-Ume

World Explorers
Senior Editor   Sean Dolan

Staff for ROBERT PEARY AND THE QUEST FOR THE NORTH POLE
Associate Editor   Terrance Dolan
Copy Editor   Christopher Duffy
Editorial Assistant   Danielle Janusz
Picture Researcher   Alan Gottlieb
Senior Designer   Basia Niemczyc

First Printing

1   3   5   7   9   8   6   4   2

Library of Congress Cataloging-in-Publication Data

Dwyer, Christopher.
Robert Peary and the Quest for the North Pole/Christopher Dwyer.
p.   cm.—(World explorers)
Includes bibliographical references and index.
Summary: Describes the history of Admiral Robert Peary's
expeditions to the North Pole, which he reached in 1909.
    ISBN 0-7910-1316-2
          0-7910-1540-8 (pbk.)
    1. Peary, Robert E. (Robert Edwin), 1856–1920—Juvenile
literature.   2. Explorers—United States—Biography—Juvenile
literature.   3. North Pole—Juvenile literature.   [1. Peary, Robert
E. (Robert Edwin), 1856–1920.   2. Explorers.   3. North Pole.]
I. Title.   II. Series.
G635.P4D85   1992   92-8446
919.804′092—dc20   CIP
[B]   AC

CONTENTS

WORLD EXPLORERS

THE EARLY EXPLORERS

Herodotus and the Explorers of the Classical Age
Marco Polo and the Medieval Explorers
The Viking Explorers

THE FIRST GREAT AGE OF DISCOVERY

Jacques Cartier, Samuel de Champlain, and the Explorers of Canada
Christopher Columbus and the First Voyages to the New World
From Coronado to Escalante: The Explorers of the Spanish Southwest
Hernando de Soto and the Explorers of the American South
Sir Francis Drake and the Struggle for an Ocean Empire
Vasco da Gama and the Portuguese Explorers
La Salle and the Explorers of the Mississippi
Ferdinand Magellan and the Discovery of the World Ocean
Pizarro, Orellana, and the Exploration of the Amazon
The Search for the Northwest Passage
Giovanni da Verrazano and the Explorers of the Atlantic Coast

THE SECOND GREAT AGE OF DISCOVERY

Roald Amundsen and the Quest for the South Pole
Daniel Boone and the Opening of the Ohio Country
Captain James Cook and the Explorers of the Pacific
The Explorers of Alaska
John Charles Frémont and the Great Western Reconnaissance
Alexander von Humboldt, Colossus of Exploration
Lewis and Clark and the Route to the Pacific
Alexander Mackenzie and the Explorers of Canada
Robert Peary and the Quest for the North Pole
Zebulon Pike and the Explorers of the American Southwest
John Wesley Powell and the Great Surveys of the American West
Jedediah Smith and the Mountain Men of the American West
Henry Stanley and the European Explorers of Africa
Lt. Charles Wilkes and the Great U.S. Exploring Expedition

THE THIRD GREAT AGE OF DISCOVERY

Apollo to the Moon
The Explorers of the Undersea World
The First Men in Space
The Mission to Mars and Beyond
Probing Deep Space

CHELSEA HOUSE PUBLISHERS

Into the Unknown

Michael Collins

It is difficult to define most eras in history with any pre-
cision, but not so the space age. On October 4, 1957, it
burst on us with little warning when the Soviet Union
launched *Sputnik*, a 184-pound cannonball that circled
the globe once every 96 minutes. Less than 4 years later,
the Soviets followed this first primitive satellite with the
flight of Yury Gagarin, a 27-year-old fighter pilot who
became the first human to orbit the earth. The Soviet
Union's success prompted President John F. Kennedy to
decide that the United States should "land a man on the
moon and return him safely to earth" before the end of
the 1960s. We now had not only a space age but a space
race.

I was born in 1930, exactly the right time to allow me
to participate in Project Apollo, as the U.S. lunar program
came to be known. As a young man growing up, I often
found myself too young to do the things I wanted—or
suddenly too old, as if someone had turned a switch at
midnight. But for Apollo, 1930 was the perfect year to be
born, and I was very lucky. In 1966 I enjoyed circling the
earth for three days, and in 1969 I flew to the moon and
laughed at the sight of the tiny earth, which I could cover
with my thumbnail.

How the early explorers would have loved the view from
space! With one glance Christopher Columbus could have
plotted his course and reassured his crew that the world

was indeed round. In 90 minutes Magellan could have looked down at every port of call in the *Victoria's* three-year circumnavigation of the globe. Given a chance to map their route from orbit, Lewis and Clark could have told President Jefferson that there was no easy Northwest Passage but that a continent of exquisite diversity awaited their scrutiny.

In a physical sense, we have already gone to most places that we can. That is not to say that there are not new adventures awaiting us deep in the sea or on the red plains of Mars, but more important than reaching new places will be understanding those we have already visited. There are vital gaps in our understanding of how our planet works as an ecosystem and how our planet fits into the infinite order of the universe. The next great age may well be the age of assimilation, in which we use microscope and telescope to evaluate what we have discovered and put that knowledge to use. The adventure of being first to reach may be replaced by the satisfaction of being first to grasp. Surely that is a form of exploration as vital to our well-being, and perhaps even survival, as the distinction of being the first to explore a specific geographical area.

The explorers whose stories are told in the books of this series did not just sail perilous seas, scale rugged mountains, traverse blistering deserts, dive to the depths of the ocean, or land on the moon. Their voyages and expeditions were journeys of mind as much as of time and distance, through which they—and all of mankind—were able to reach a greater understanding of our universe. That challenge remains, for all of us. The imperative is to see, to understand, to develop knowledge that others can use, to help nurture this planet that sustains us all. Perhaps being born in 1975 will be as lucky for a new generation of explorer as being born in 1930 was for Neil Armstrong, Buzz Aldrin, and Mike Collins.

The Reader's Journey

William H. Goetzmann

This volume is one of a series that takes us with the great explorers of the ages on bold journeys over the oceans and the continents and into outer space. As we travel along with these imaginative and courageous journeyers, we share their adventures and their knowledge. We also get a glimpse of that mysterious and inextinguishable fire that burned in the breast of men such as Magellan and Columbus—the fire that has propelled all those throughout the ages who have been driven to leave behind family and friends for a voyage into the unknown.

No one has ever satisfactorily explained the urge to explore, the drive to go to the "back of beyond." It is certain that it has been present in man almost since he began walking erect and first ventured across the African savannas. Sparks from that same fire fueled the transoceanic explorers of the Ice Age, who led their people across the vast plain that formed a land bridge between Asia and North America, and the astronauts and scientists who determined that man must reach the moon.

Besides an element of adventure, all exploration involves an element of mystery. We must not confuse exploration with discovery. Exploration is a purposeful human activity—a search for something. Discovery may be the end result of that search; it may also be an accident,

as when Columbus found a whole new world while searching for the Indies. Often, the explorer may not even realize
the full significance of what he has discovered, as was the
case with Columbus. Exploration, on the other hand, is
the product of a cultural or individual curiosity; it is a
unique process that has enabled mankind to know and
understand the world's oceans, continents, and polar regions. It is at the heart of scientific thinking. One of its
most significant aspects is that it teaches people to ask the
right questions; by doing so, it forces us to reevaluate what
we think we know and understand. Thus knowledge pro-
gresses, and we are driven constantly to a new awareness
and appreciation of the universe in all its infinite variety.

The motivation for exploration is not always pure. In
his fascination with the new, man often forgets that others
have been there before him. For example, the popular
notion of the discovery of America overlooks the complex
Indian civilizations that had existed there for thousands of
years before the arrival of Europeans. Man's desire for
conquest, riches, and fame is often linked inextricably with
his quest for the unknown, but a story that touches so
closely on the human essence must of necessity treat war
as well as peace, avarice with generosity, both pride and
humility, frailty and greatness. The story of exploration is
above all a story of humanity and of man's understanding
of his place in the universe.

The WORLD EXPLORERS series has been divided into four
sections. The first treats the explorers of the ancient world,
the Viking explorers of the 9th through the 11th centuries,
and Marco Polo and the medieval explorers. The rest of
the series is divided into three great ages of exploration.
The first is the era of Columbus and Magellan: the period
spanning the 15th and 16th centuries, which saw the discovery and exploration of the New World and the world
ocean. The second might be called the age of science and
imperialism, the era made possible by the scientific ad-
vances of the 17th century, which witnessed the discovery

of the world's last two undiscovered continents, Australia and Antarctica, the mapping of all the continents and oceans, and the establishment of colonies all over the world. The third great age refers to the most ambitious quests of the 20th century—the probing of space and of the ocean's depths.

As we reach out into the darkness of outer space and other galaxies, we come to better understand how our ancestors confronted *oecumene,* or the vast earthly unknown. We learn once again the meaning of an unknown 18th-century sea captain's advice to navigators:

> And if by chance you make a landfall on the shores of another sea in a far country inhabited by savages and barbarians, remember you this: the greatest danger and the surest hope lies not with fires and arrows but in the quicksilver hearts of men.

At its core, exploration is a series of moral dramas. But it is these dramas, involving new lands, new people, and exotic ecosystems of staggering beauty, that make the explorers' stories not only moral tales but also some of the greatest adventure stories ever recorded. They represent the process of learning in its most expansive and vivid forms. We see that real life, past and present, transcends even the adventures of the starship *Enterprise.*

These
Arctic Fellows

I'll get to Conger before Sverdrup if it kills me!" Lieutenant Robert Peary shouted in December 1898, believing that one of his rivals in the race to the North Pole, the Norwegian explorer Captain Otto Sverdrup, intended to occupy Fort Conger, a tiny Arctic outpost located on the coast of Ellesmere Island, the northernmost landmass in Canada. Fort Conger lay within striking distance of the Arctic Ocean, and Peary had planned to use it as a winter quarters and a base camp from which to mount an assault on the North Pole. But his ship, the *Windward*, had become icebound in Kane Basin, 250 miles south of Fort Conger. And now Peary, learning that Sverdrup was also icebound, just 43 miles south of the *Windward*, was convinced that his Norwegian rival was going to steal a march on him to Fort Conger.

Peary decided on a preemptive hike. He informed his physician, Dr. T. S. Dedrick; his longtime assistant, Matthew Henson; and four Inuits who were part of the expedition to prepare themselves, the dogs, and the sledges for an immediate journey to Fort Conger. Dedrick and Henson (not to mention the Inuits) were appalled; it was the dead of winter and such a march might very well kill them. But Peary had in his eye the cold, almost savage glint with which Henson and the doctor had become exceedingly familiar, and soon the seven men had left the

Most polar explorers were exceptionally driven men but even among this obsessed fraternity Robert Peary's monomaniacal intensity made him unique.

relative comfort and safety of the ship behind and were sledging north through the perpetual night of the Arctic winter.

It proved to be a nightmarish trek across a nocturnal landscape of towering snowdrifts and jagged ice ridges. Blizzards howled, and there were times during the 2-week march when the temperature dipped below minus 50 degrees Fahrenheit. About three days short of their destination, two of the Inuits, exhausted and frightened, would go no farther. They were left behind with nine of the dogs. On January 6, the remaining members of the party sighted the forlorn huts of Fort Conger, which had been built by members of the doomed Greely expedition 16 years before. The place looked every bit an outpost at the edge of the world, which in fact it was, haunted by earlier Arctic disasters.

Once his men were safely inside one of the huts and had managed to start a fire, Peary, bothered by a "wooden feeling" in his feet, asked Henson to help him take off his boots. After the boots were removed, Henson peeled off the lieutenant's rabbit-skin socks. There was a cracking sound. Peary looked at his feet in surprise. Most of his toes had come off with the rabbit skin. Frozen solid, they had simply snapped off like twigs. "My God, Lieutenant!" Henson exclaimed in horror. "Why didn't you tell me your feet were frozen?" Examining his mutilated feet,

Peary and his men set off by dogsled from the icebound Windward. In the course of his many attempts at the North Pole, Peary would become the foremost dogsled traveler of his day.

The American Arctic. Peary considered the Smith Sound route to northernmost Greenland and Ellesmere Island and onward across the ice to the North Pole to be "preeminently the American route."

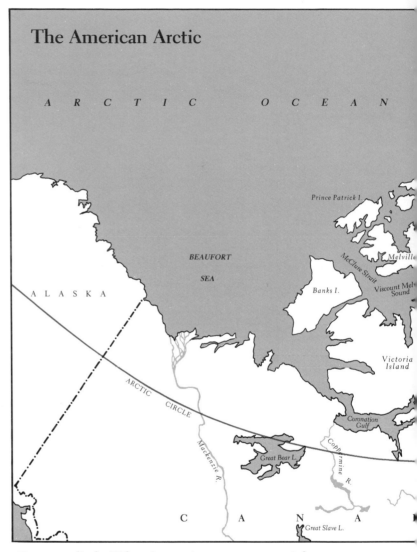

The American Arctic

A R C T I C   O C E A N

Prince Patrick I.

BEAUFORT

SEA

McClure Strait

Melville

ALASKA

Banks I.

Viscount Mel Sound

ARCTIC CIRCLE

Victoria Island

Coronation Gulf

Mackenzie R.

Great Bear L.

Coppermine R.

C   A   N   A

Great Slave L.

Peary replied, "There's no time to pamper sick men on the trail. Besides, a few toes aren't much to give to achieve the Pole."

"The Pole," as Peary called it, was the North Pole, the northernmost point on the earth, located at the top of the globe at 90 degrees north latitude atop the ice-covered Arctic Ocean. For Robert Peary and the other explorers who were willing to suffer untold miseries—and to risk a

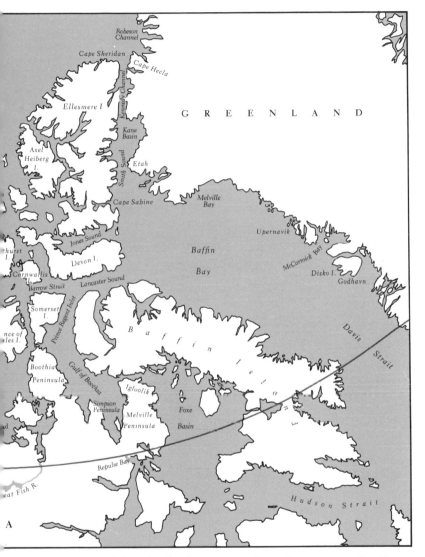

cold and lonely death—to get there first, it was the "last great geographical prize."

Mariners had been testing their ships in the frigid, iceberg-haunted waters of the Far North for centuries, probing for the Northwest Passage, a commercial sea route through the Canadian Arctic Islands that was believed to connect the Atlantic and the Pacific. In 1607, the legendary English (though he was then sailing for Holland) navigator Henry Hudson, while searching for the Passage, attempted to sail across the top of the world. Although he failed to do so, Hudson reached a latitude of 80 degrees north in the waters west of Spitsbergen, the Arctic island lying due north of Norway. (On a subsequent voyage, three years later, Hudson and his young son were set adrift in Hudson Bay in a small boat by a mutinous crew and never seen again.) Hudson's farthest north was not bested until 1773, when Captain Constantine Phipps of the Royal Navy managed to push his ship a few miles closer to the Pole before he was stopped by the ice pack of the Arctic Ocean.

By the end of the 18th century, the Northwest Passage had yet to be found, but by then the concept of the North

Pole as an objective in itself had begun to take on a new significance. The British government in particular was starting to view the Pole as a valuable symbolic and strategic prize that would add to national prestige and also give Great Britain a leg up on their foreign rivals in the north. In 1826, therefore, Lieutenant William Edward Parry (usually referred to as Edward), an ambitious Royal Navy officer and veteran of three failed Northwest Passage attempts, proposed an expedition to reach the North Pole. Parry's proposal was unique; instead of trying to sail directly all the way to the Pole, as had previous explorers, he would force his ships as far north of Spitsbergen as possible, after which the expedition members would proceed on foot over the Arctic ice pack to the Pole.

William Edward Parry's 1827 expedition, the first to attempt to reach the North Pole by crossing the ice on foot, was also the first to experience the demoralizing effect of the ice's tendency to drift.

Although Parry was the first white explorer to actually mount a walking expedition across the Arctic Ocean, the concept had been around for a while. Parry himself had gotten the idea from a fellow Arctic explorer, John Franklin, who, along with other men who had pushed their vessels to the eastern edge of the Arctic Ocean, had seen that the ice north of Spitsbergen appeared to be remarkably flat and solid. Parry believed he could traverse the ice pack and make it to the Pole during the relatively mild Arctic summer.

On June 21, 1827, Parry led a company of 25 men onto the ice pack. The team was equipped with 2 large boats, which were fitted with steel runners so they could also act as sledges, and 71 days of provisions. This first encounter with the Arctic Ocean was brief and bitter. The flat, solid ice Parry had expected was nowhere to be found. Instead, the men labored over a rough, uneven ice pack that was melting and breaking up under the summer sun, slogging through ankle-deep slush and around pressure ridges that were up to 40 feet high. At the numerous large gaps in the ice—called leads—Parry's men took to their boats and rowed across, then hauled the boats back up onto the ice and toiled onward, dragging the boats along behind them. It rained constantly, thick fogs engulfed them, and sharp ice mangled their footwear; and the ice pack continued to break up like a great jigsaw puzzle coming apart.

As the weeks wore on, Parry discovered an invisible, implacable adversary—a strong wind from the Pole that was pushing the ice rapidly south. He and his men, laboring northward, found themselves on an Arctic treadmill. By July 28, although they had traveled 978 miles, the company was actually only 178 miles north of their point of origin. A discouraged Parry called a halt to the expedition at 82 degrees north latitude. This was a new farthest north, but they were still more than 400 miles away from the Pole.

Rebuffed by the Pole, the British once again turned their attention to the Northwest Passage. With a remarkable tenacity and an even more remarkable foolhardiness, they sent ships, one after another and sometimes two or three at a time, into the treacherous labyrinth of waterways that separate the islands of the Canadian Arctic. "They cannot help it, these Arctic fellows," commented one observer. "It is in the blood." Disaster followed upon disaster, but the officers of the Royal Navy, unperturbed and refusing to make any tactical concessions to what was obviously an inhospitable environment, went bravely forth. A good number of them never came back. In 1845, Sir John Franklin, then a plump, amiable 60-year-old, sailed 2 ships with a crew of 134 men into the Canadian Arctic in search of the Northwest Passage. The two ships vanished, taking with them all hands aboard.

Now, along with the Pole and the Passage, there was a new prize in the Arctic—Sir John. Large rewards were offered to anyone who could discover any information concerning the missing Englishman and his crew. For the next 20 years, Britain sent a continuous stream of ships to the Arctic in search of the missing explorers. American expeditions joined the hunt. No less than 50 rescue missions were launched between 1850 and 1875. The search for Franklin often resembled an Arctic comedy of errors. There were times when the ships of several different expeditions found themselves icebound for the winter in the same bay or channel. More than once, rescue expeditions were dispatched to find lost rescue expeditions. There were new Arctic debacles, and many of the searchers found death in the frozen wastes. But nobody found Franklin.

By 1859, relics of the doomed Franklin expedition—including a skeleton—had been found scattered along a desolate beach on King William Island. It was apparent that Franklin and his men had abandoned their icebound ships and then perished from exposure, starvation, and scurvy during a desperate overland march. The great

Searchers uncover the skeletons of two of the men of the Franklin expedition. The disastrous last expedition of Sir John Franklin, in which two huge British warships were swallowed up by the Arctic ice and all hands aboard met a frigid, grisly death from starvation, scurvy, and exposure, was the greatest of Britain's polar misadventures.

search never did turn up Franklin's body, but it was not an altogether quixotic and unproductive venture. One of the searchers, Robert McClure, discovered a potential Northwest Passage during the hunt for the missing men. Much of the previously unmapped south Arctic was charted by members of the rescue expeditions, and the search also resulted in the accumulation of practical knowledge about exploring and surviving in the Arctic. Those men who were still inclined to make an attempt at the Pole knew well what kind of obstacles they would have to overcome. The Arctic was clearly the most pitiless, unforgiving environment on earth.

A variety of elements combined to make the Arctic a graveyard for explorers. The weather and the Arctic terrain posed the most obvious dangers. In the summer months, the temperature rarely exceeded 40 degrees. In the fall and winter, especially during the long Arctic night, it was a place of bone-chilling, skin-freezing, unrelenting cold. (Because of the far-northern latitude of the Arctic region, the sun sets in the early winter and does not reappear again until spring. During the ensuing Arctic summer, the sun remains above the horizon 24 hours a day.) Freezing northern winds and blizzards exacerbated the chilly conditions. Frostbite and hypothermia were constant threats.

No other place on earth had such a profoundly depressing and demoralizing psychological effect on the humans who traveled through it. *Desolation* is the word most frequently used by Arctic explorers to describe that environment. To be trapped in that region during the ceaseless darkness of the Arctic winter was an experience that could change an explorer forever. Many men who were able to survive the physical dangers—scurvy and other illnesses, malnutrition, frostbite, hypothermia, polar bears—were undone psychologically. "The very soul of man seems to be suffocated by the oppressive gloom," one adventurer wrote. Hallucinations and delusions would occur. Beset by severe depression—what the explorers referred to as the "blue devils"—Arctic travelers would become listless and irritable. Some would even develop homicidal or suicidal tendencies. The American explorer Isaac Hayes wrote that the dark and silent Arctic night "oppresses the understanding, and the desolation, which everywhere reigns, haunts the imagination; the silence—dark, dreary, and profound—becomes a terror."

And then there was the ice, the archenemy of the Arctic explorer. "To us," wrote the Scotsman John Ross, a veteran of several British expeditions to the Arctic, "the ice was a plague, a vexation, a torment, an evil, a matter of despair." There was no escaping it, for the Far North was a world of ice. From the ancient ice of the Arctic Ocean and the glaciers, to the great icebergs and ice floes that choked the channels and bays and straits of the Arctic Archipelago, to the permafrost that covered the northernmost islands, the ice was omnipresent. The ice surrounded and entrapped ships, bullied them, attacked them, laid siege to them, held them fast in a frozen grip for months at a time, pushed them this way and that, towered above them and threatened them from below, shrugged them out of the water and left them beached, tipped them over, chewed them up and spit them out in splinters.

Those explorers who traveled, by choice or necessity, on foot—and especially those who attempted to cross the Arctic Ocean ice pack—were bedeviled as well. Out there the elements and currents formed the ice into a slippery, craggy, tortuous terrain that could reshape itself in a matter of hours. It was like a living thing—treacherous, always moving, shifting beneath the travelers' feet, carrying them backward when they wanted to go forward, west when they

wanted to go east, and every once in a while it simply opened up beneath a man and swallowed him whole. An entire sledge, with its dog team and driver, might vanish in the blink of an eye.

Once it became clear that Franklin and his men had indeed perished, Great Britain began a gradual but steady withdrawal from the Arctic, which had claimed so many English ships and English lives. They would leave the crusade for the North Pole to the reckless Americans, the stubborn Norwegians, the stolid Swedes, and anybody else who was foolish enough to try. By 1875, when the last British attempt at the Pole failed, most knowledgeable Englishmen believed the last great geographic prize to be about as attainable as the moon.

The wintry Arctic night descends on the Hecla *and the* Griper, *the ships commanded by Parry in 1819 on his first Arctic expedition, a failed attempt at the Northwest Passage. In the course of the voyage, Parry and his men became the first whites to winter in the Arctic Archipelago and the first practitioners of the foolhardy British method of transport known as manhauling.*

Thank God Harbor

Robert Edwin Peary was born to Charles and Mary Peary in the small town of Cresson, Pennsylvania, on May 6, 1856. The boy never had a chance to know his father, who died of pneumonia two and a half years later. His mother was somewhat overprotective of her son; she was to remain so even when Peary had become a celebrated adventurer and a survivor of years of exploration in the bleak and dangerous Far North. As an only child, young Peary was a loner. He had few playmates and found companionship instead in books and in nature. He was a serious little fellow, a preadolescent naturalist who liked to take long exploratory hikes through the woods.

At age 9, Peary was packed off to a boarding school in Topsham, Maine, which he attended until he was 16. There he established himself as an exemplary student and spent his free time studying taxidermy and hiking through the White Mountains and the countryside around Casco Bay, but he was an oddly discontented youth. He felt in some way different from his peers; he would always feel that way. He was troubled by a vague restlessness, a feeling that he was somehow meant to do something more, something extraordinary, although he could not say what it was to be. Though he had some friends at the boarding school, for the most part he remained aloof and alienated from his fellow students, preferring long, solitary walks in the forest to social events.

Peary as a young man at Bowdoin College, where a professor of civil engineering named George Leonard Vose often discussed the possibility of reaching the North Pole with a number of support teams as an exercise in problem solving.

Mary Peary, the explorer's mother. Peary's father died while he was still an infant, and the relationship between mother and only son subsequently became exceptionally close. According to Fitzhugh Green, one of Peary's early biographers, "living alone with his mother probably did more to make [Peary] a great explorer than any other single factor."

In 1873, Peary was admitted to exclusive Bowdoin College, in Brunswick, Maine. He moved into an off-campus apartment with his mother, who was ill. Although they considered this arrangement to be a little strange, Peary's collegiate peers, as well as his instructors, came to admire and respect him. He had a girlfriend, Mary Kilby, and he pursued a degree in civil engineering. Peary had grown to be a handsome and healthy young man. In his own words, he was "tall, erect, broad-shouldered, full-chested, tough, wiry-limbed, clear-eyed, full mustached, clear-browed, a dead shot, a powerful, tireless swimmer, a first-class rider and a skillful boxer and fencer." Although he was still restless and occasionally depressed, his years at Bowdoin were good ones. It was during this time that Robert Peary began thinking seriously about the two things that would come to dominate his existence, although for him they were one in the same—fame and the North Pole.

It is not surprising that a young American who sought celebrity and adventure in the late 19th century would see the North Pole as a way to attain them. Such thoughts are similar to the aspirations of young men and women of the late 20th century who dream of becoming astronauts and taking part in the exploration of outer space. Successful Arctic explorers were treated in much the same way as astronauts such as John Glenn and Neil Armstrong were treated following their historic spaceflights; they were international heroes who were given parades and invited to dinner with presidents and other heads of state, after which they would make substantial amounts of money by going on lecture tours and by writing best-sellers based on their experiences. During Peary's childhood and throughout the following years, Arctic exploration, including a succession of dramatic and tragic attempts by Americans to reach the North Pole, was ongoing, and tales of the thrilling exploits of the explorers filled the newspapers and bookstores of the day. Perhaps the most widely read of these accounts (in the United States, at least) was Elisha Kent Kane's *Arctic Explorations*, published in 1857. Peary read it as a boy and much later in life remembered it as a "wonderful book."

Dr. Elisha Kent Kane of Philadelphia was one of the first Americans to go to the Arctic. He was a boastful, flamboyant character, a compulsive adventurer who had traveled much of the globe. Kane went north in 1850 as ship's surgeon for the first American expedition to the Pole, which was sponsored by the New York shipping tycoon Henry Grinnell, who was also president of the American Geographical Society. Kane was captivated by the pristine

Dr. Elisha Kent Kane was the first polar explorer to live and travel with the Inuit. Kane was the rebellious scion of a prominent Philadelphia family; his penchant for adventure owed in part to his knowledge that an untreatable heart condition made it likely that he would die young.

beauty of the Arctic, and upon returning to the United States he convinced Grinnell to finance another expedition, which Kane himself would lead. The ostensible goal of the second expedition was also to find Franklin, but Kane told Grinnell that if it was possible, he would make a dash for the Pole.

In 1853, Kane and a crew of 17 set sail in the 144-ton *Advance*, a relatively small ship for Arctic waters. Kane had decided to follow the western, or Smith Sound, route rather than a more easterly route by way of Spitsbergen. In 1616, English navigator William Baffin had sailed north along the west coast of Greenland into a gigantic bay that was enclosed to the west by an immense island. The island and the bay bear Baffin's name today. Continuing up the Greenland coast, Baffin discovered and named three sounds. One of them—Smith Sound—extended directly north between Greenland and Ellesmere Island. More than two centuries later, Kane took the *Advance* northward through Smith Sound to what is known today as Kane Basin. At the south end of the basin, the *Advance* met the ice for the first time. The ship was stopped cold, and the expedition wintered in nearby Rensselaer Harbor on the Greenland coast.

Kane spent the winter planning his assault on the Pole. In the spring, he hoped to use sledge dogs, which he had obtained from Inuits at the Greenland settlements of Upernavik and Etah, to drive up Greenland's coastline to the Arctic Ocean. Using dogs was a radical departure from the traditional—and extremely silly—British practice of "manhauling" sledges in the Arctic, and it would prove to be the single most important adaptation of Inuit ways made by Arctic explorers. These remarkable animals would eventually carry the first man to the North Pole, but they would not get Elisha Kane there. Unfortunately for Kane, his dogs died of a nervous disorder, and he was not able to obtain more before spring. Kane was nevertheless determined to plant the Stars and Stripes at the

Pole. In early March, against the advice of the party's dog-team driver, Danish Greenlander Carl Petersen, who believed that it was too early in the season for Arctic travel, Kane sent an advance party north.

Petersen was correct—it was too early to travel. The eight members of the advance party—including Petersen—dragged their heavy sledge through a raging blizzard. The temperature dropped to 40 degrees below zero. The advance party turned back, but only Petersen and two others made it to the ship. Kane then led a rescue party in search of the others, who were found huddled in a little tent, slowly freezing to death. Kane roused the groggy men, who were on the verge of slipping into hypothermic coma. Those who could not walk were strapped to sledges, and they started back toward the *Advance*. The return journey was so grueling that one of the rescuers, a hardened New York harbor boatman named William Godfrey, found himself contemplating suicide as he labored over the ice.

Isaac Hayes, who had been left behind to mind the ship, was sickened by the party of frozen, walking corpses that materialized out of the Arctic dusk and clambered stiffly aboard. All of them, including Kane, seemed to have gone insane. Their teeth chattered crazily, and they babbled and wept and stared wildly about as if they did not know where they were. Soon, according to Hayes, the *Advance* "presented all the appearances of a mad house." As a result of Kane's "attempt" at the Pole, two of the men died, and most of the others lost bits of their toes and fingers to frostbite.

Although some valuable exploration was done in May, when the 60-mile-long Humboldt Glacier, Kennedy Channel, and Cape Constitution were discovered, Kane's expedition deteriorated steadily. To his horror, the ice in Rensselaer Harbor did not melt during the summer, and as winter closed in again and it became clear to the crew that the *Advance* would remain icebound, tensions

mounted, for the thought of another dark winter in the
Arctic was too much for most of the party to handle. Kane
came to blows with some of the men, including the tough
Godfrey. Twelve members of the expedition deserted the
ship and started marching south; Kane, with his last glass
of sherry, toasted them sarcastically as they wandered off
across the ice, knowing they would return—which they

Kane's men haul a sledge across a gaping crevasse in the ice. The illustration is from his Arctic Explorations, *which Peary read as young boy and remembered as a "wonderful book."*

did. Eventually, Kane was reduced to eating the rats that infested the ship, for they were the only available source of fresh meat, and fresh meat, which contains vitamin C, was needed to ward off the ravages of scurvy. The others, who refused to eat the rats, found themselves racked by the debilitating disease. For fuel, they burned the ship piece by piece, saving only the two whaleboats. In the spring of 1855, Kane and his desperate crew, with the help of Inuits from Etah, dragged the boats 90 miles over the ice to open water. Forty-nine days later, after a harrowing journey beneath the towering, glittering ice cliffs of Baffin Bay, they were rescued by a whaler.

Kane returned to civilization as an international hero, and soon his sensational written accounts of his Arctic adventures were being read everywhere. In Cincinnati, Ohio, a short, stocky, poorly educated, small-time newspaper publisher named Charles Francis Hall was caught up in the new wave of interest in the Arctic. He began writing editorials calling for another American attempt at the North Pole. AMERICANS CAN DO IT, his newpaper declared. In fact, Hall began to think, *he* could do it. He abruptly sold his newspaper and, leaving his wife and children behind, traveled to New York to raise money for an expedition to the Arctic. Potential contributors, learning that Hall had never been farther north than the Bronx and had prepared for his expedition by camping out for a few

Kane's men sullenly await their meal to be ready. Kane is seated, third from left, closest to the simmering kettle; Isaac Hayes is standing, second from left. For many North Pole expeditions, the enforced isolation and monotony of an Arctic winter was as great an enemy as the numbing cold.

This illustration of Charles Francis Hall with two Inuit friends served as the frontispiece for the published edition of his Arctic journals. Many of his contemporaries regarded Hall as slightly mad, but his determination to learn the Inuit ways of coping with their frigid environment made him one of the most remarkable Arctic explorers.

nights in a tent, were not forthcoming. This did not bother Hall, who simply hitched a ride on a whaling ship and went to the Arctic, alone. Thus began nine years of unprecedented Arctic exploration. Robert Peary, who was just four years old when Hall first went north, would eventually study the accounts of many of the Arctic explorers who preceded him, but the actions of the improbable Charles Francis Hall would have the greatest impact on his own Arctic career.

The whaler *George Henry* dropped Hall off at Baffin Island in August 1860. Most of the whaling men thought that Hall was a crackpot, for no white man had ever attempted to live alone in the Arctic. But Hall had already formed his own ideas about survival in the Far North, and he immediately put them to the test. It was his belief that a white explorer in the Arctic must learn to thoroughly "Esquimeaux-ise himself," as he put it, so he promptly moved into an Inuit village on the island and did just that. While living in an igloo with an Inuit family, Hall adopted their way of life. (*Inuit* is what the people of the Arctic call themselves; *Eskimo* was originally adopted by the British from a derogatory Indian name for the Inuit. Hall was the first to use the term *Inuit* in his writings.) He replaced his woolen clothes with Inuit-style furs and sealskin, which retained warmth and repelled moisture more efficiently. He learned how to hunt like the natives, and he ate Inuit food—raw seal and whale meat, whale blubber, and aged, uncooked caribou meat, among other things. Hall also studied the difficult skill of sled-dog driving. Not surprisingly, the white man thrived, for the Inuit way was finely attuned to the harsh Arctic environment. He ranged far and wide from his quarters on Baffin Island, in the process finding numerous artifacts that had been left in the Arctic nearly 300 years earlier by an expedition led by Martin Frobisher, an English mariner who sailed in search of the Northwest Passage.

Hall returned to the United States to find the nation engulfed in the Civil War. He was disgusted. "Away with politics," he commented, and by 1865 he was back among the Inuit, living in an ice house at Repulse Bay, an inlet, just at the latitude of the Arctic Circle, on the east coast of the Melville Peninsula, which is immediately northwest of Hudson Bay. Once Hall was sufficiently re-Esquimeaux-ised, he decided to join the never-ending hunt for survivors of the Franklin expedition. On King William Island, which he reached after sledging westward across the Melville, Simpson, and Boothia peninsulas and the frozen gulfs that separated them, he discovered sad relics from the lost expedition scattered along the beach. There was silverware, books, coins, pieces of furniture from

Franklin's ships, and the occasional bleached skeleton lying where it had dropped decades ago, with scraps of Royal Navy wool still clinging to the bones. Many of the local Inuit remembered or had heard of the passage of the doomed company. The Englishmen had been riddled with scurvy and half mad from starvation. Behind them they dragged heavy sledges filled with useless items from their abandoned ships. They begged the Inuits for food, but the natives were frightened by their ghastly appearance and would not approach. Hall spent the summer of 1868 collecting artifacts and mulling over these dark tales, which had already become part of Inuit folk history. In 1869, after an unparalleled five consecutive years in the Arctic, he returned once again to the United States.

Upon returning to the States, Hall found that he was no longer regarded as an obscure and eccentric Far North wanderer. Instead, he was lionized in America—much as Kane had been—as one of the foremost Arctic explorers of his day. He wasted no time putting his newfound fame to work. All of the long, lonely months he had spent in

An Inuit winter village, from Hall's Life Among the Eskimos. *"I have always held the opinion that whoever would lead the way there should have first have years of experience among the wild natives of the North," Hall wrote about the quest for the North Pole.*

Dr. Emil Bessels, who certified Hall's cause of death as stroke and laughingly commented that his untimely demise was the best thing that could have happened to the expedition, remains the prime suspect in Hall's death, although there is no logical motive for the alleged murder.

the Arctic up to that point, he informed anyone who would listen (including President Ulysses S. Grant), had merely been training for an attempt at the North Pole. Hall was convinced that he was the man to achieve the Pole, and so were a lot of other people. He was given a grant of $50,000 by the Senate Appropriations Committee, and in June 1871 the 387-ton *Polaris*, reinforced for the rigors of Arctic travel, steamed northward. Charles Francis Hall was no longer a lone traveler; now he found himself in command of a large government-funded expedition. With him were Captain Sidney Budington, an experienced whaler; Captain George Tyson, serving as first mate; Dr. Emil Bessels, a German who had been to the Arctic previously; and an Inuit contingent.

The sturdy *Polaris* surpassed Kane's farthest north by 200 miles, pushing up through Smith Sound and Kennedy Channel to what is known today as Hall Basin. From there, Hall sledged to within sight of the frozen polar sea, but that was as far north as he would ever go. After returning to the ship from a sledge journey one day, Hall drank a cup of coffee and became violently ill. He said that his stomach was burning and retired to his cabin; soon he was feverish and apparently delirious. He believed someone had poisoned him; a week later he was dead. Dr. Bessels determined that Hall had died of a stroke. The crew buried him on the Greenland shore, at a place Hall had named Thank God Harbor.

But was it a stroke? Some members of the expedition later expressed their doubts about this diagnosis and suggested that Hall had been murdered. The expedition had been beset by jealousy and dissension from the beginning, and by the time the Arctic night had fallen over Kennedy Channel, tensions were dangerously high. The German, Dr. Bessels, had grown to hate Hall, and the feeling was apparently mutual. Hall was by no means an easy man to get along with. He had a large ego, a brusque manner, and a volatile temper. Several years earlier, back at Repulse

Bessels drew this eyewitness sketch of Hall's burial at Thank God Harbor. If Hall was indeed murdered, the true culprit may have been the intense psychological pressures of the dark Arctic winter. Noah Hayes, a member of the last Hall expedition, believed "that no man can retain the use of his faculties through one long night to such a degree as to be morally responsible . . . for all that he may say and do."

Bay, he had lost his temper with a whaler and had subsequently shot and killed the man. Perhaps a similar fate had befallen him aboard the *Polaris*. Dark thoughts and violent confrontations were not uncommon among groups of men trapped together in close quarters during the bleak months of the Arctic winter.

In 1968, Hall's biographer, Chauncey Loomis, believing that the symptoms Hall manifested shortly before his death resembled those of arsenic poisoning, obtained permission to have the explorer disinterred. Hall's corpse was freed from its icy grave and examined. It was determined that Hall had indeed been poisoned; tissue samples showed that he had ingested toxic amounts of arsenic shortly before he died. Who poisoned Charles Francis Hall? And why? Nobody will ever know. As poet Robert W. Service, the self-styled bard of the Far North, wrote: "The Arctic trails have their secret tales that would make your blood run cold."

Cape Sabine

In 1876, Robert Peary graduated from Bowdoin College, ranked second in a class of 52, with a degree in civil engineering. He then moved to the town of Fryeburg, Maine, with his mother. There was not much need for civil engineers in little Fryeburg, however, so Peary set himself up as a mail-order taxidermist. Although he made a decent living, he was soon restless and dissatisfied again. Stuffing birds in a New England backwater was not his idea of an adventurous life, and he yearned for something more. "How many have wished and wondered about the mysterious future as I do?" he wrote in a letter to Mary Kilby.

In 1878, Peary saw a notice in the local post office announcing four vacancies for the position of draftsman in the U.S. Coast and Geodetic Survey in Washington, D.C. For Peary, this unobtrusive notice tacked to the post-office bulletin board represented a chance to escape Fryeburg. He did not waste the opportunity, mailing in an impressive application that included his own survey of Fryeburg. He was accepted for one of the available positions, and in July 1879, at the age of 23, he reported for work at the Coast Survey Building on Capitol Hill. (His mother remained in Maine.) But it did not take long for Peary's initial enthusiasm and excitement at the novelty of his situation to wear off.

Hunched over a desk in a small office day after day, Peary felt like a "machine." In a letter to his mother, he

Peary first went to Nicaragua in 1885. Initially, he believed that the survey for a canal route across Nicaragua offered as great an opportunity for fame as did the quest for the North Pole. The discovery of a viable route for a canal connecting the Atlantic and the Pacific would leave him "laden with glory which shall make the name of its discoverer the equal of any since history began," he wrote in a letter to his mother.

wrote that he was "overmastered by a resistless desire to do something . . . . Here I am, 24 years old, and what have I done? Nothing." He imagined himself a great explorer and conqueror like Christopher Columbus or Hernán Cortés. Recalling his long hikes through the White Mountains, he wrote, "I have stood upon the summit of a mountain after a long day's climb through woods and over rocks and, looking toward the setting sun, have given my imagination full sway until I know I have felt something of that same thrill that Cortez felt when at the close of that beautiful spring day he gained the summit of that last range of mountains that lay between him and the city of the Aztecs and, looking westward, saw the valley nestling in the rays of the sun and the mysterious city glistening in the midst of its surrounding lakes."

By 1881, Robert Peary had had enough of his deskbound existence. Despite the protests of his mother, he applied for a commission as a civil engineer in the U.S. Navy, a decision that would change his life forever and set him on a path toward those things he had dreamed about during his long, lonely woodland hikes in Maine and those interminable afternoons at his drafting table in the nation's capital. As a navy engineer, Peary came into his own, and things began to fall into place for him. He quickly impressed his superiors and made a name for himself as a skilled and hardworking engineer. In 1882, he was stationed at the U.S. Naval Station at Key West, Florida. There, he tackled the formidable task of designing and building a new pier for the station. He enjoyed the challenge and his new responsibilities. "It's different from the Coast Survey," he wrote to his mother. "I am Boss instead of bossed, have a room of my own, [and] have over a hundred men under my control." While he was at work on the pier, Peary began to court Josephine Diebitsch, the beautiful daughter of a professor at the Smithsonian Institution, whom he had first met at a dance in Washington. (Mary Kilby, his former girlfriend, seems to

"If she does not love me with her whole heart, then she is a most consummate and consistent actress," Peary wrote to his mother about his beloved, Josephine Diebitsch, on September 18, 1887. *"I shall take the risk and within the week ask her to marry me."* He would never have reason to doubt *"Jo's"* commitment to him.

have fallen by the wayside.) Soon Peary and Josephine were engaged to be married.

In 1885, Peary's hard work in Florida paid off; he was assigned to work on a geographic survey for a proposed canal to be built across Nicaragua between the Pacific and Atlantic oceans. (Though the canal was eventually built, it was constructed in Panama rather than Nicaragua.) Here was his first opportunity for travel and true adventure in an alien and hostile environment. In the sweltering, fetid

Peary (at center, in sun helmet) in Nicaragua with his surveying crew. His three months in Nicaragua in 1885 were spent "cutting, lifting, pushing, swimming" through jungle and swamps; there was "scar[c]ely a place where fifty feet could be gained without cutting or clearing away a log or lifting a boat over one."

Nicaraguan jungle, Peary's stamina and resourcefulness, as well as his leadership abilities, were tested for the first time. He thrived in this role, and when he returned to Washington, D.C., and Josephine three months later, Lieutenant Peary was sporting a deep tan, a bristling handlebar mustache, and an abundance of self-confidence.

Peary's Arctic dreams had not faded away during the Fryeburg years or during his time at the U.S. Coast Survey, nor had he allowed them to melt away under the hot Florida sun or in the humid Central American jungles. He would not allow his success in the navy to obscure them or render them obsolete, nor would he allow his impending marriage to make them seem impractical; his future bride would soon learn that Peary was married to the Arctic as surely as he was wed to her. He had kept his dreams close to his heart and had nurtured them. He continued to read everything he could get his hands on about the Arctic and Arctic exploration, and he followed with an almost obsessive attention the accounts in the newspapers of the latest attempts at the North Pole.

The last British polar expedition had been undertaken in 1876 under the command of George Nares of the Royal Navy. Although he established a new farthest north of 83 degrees north latitude, Nares, like all the other Britishers, had failed to reach the Pole, and the field was left to the hellbent Americans. In July 1879, while Peary toiled at his drafting table in Washington, D.C., a U.S. expedition, financed by New York *Herald* publisher James Gordon Bennett and led by U.S. Navy veteran Lieutenant George Washington De Long, got under way. Unlike Kane and Hall, De Long planned to make his assault on the Pole by way of the Bering Strait and Wrangel Land, an island in the East Siberian Sea, where he believed he would encounter relatively ice free waters warmed by a mild "Japanese current" that supposedly flowed northward from the Pacific Ocean through the Bering Strait.

Accordingly, De Long piloted his vessel, the 420-ton *Jeannette*, up through the Bering Strait, toward and then around Wrangel Land, and directly into the Arctic ice pack, which took hold of the *Jeannette* and refused to let go. The *Jeannette* and her crew were held captive by the ice for 22 months. The ship was at the mercy of the drifting ice pack, which carried it west past Wrangel Land and then northwest along the Siberian coastline. In the ship's log, De Long wrote that the *Jeannette* was "drifting about like a modern Flying Dutchman, never getting anywhere, but always restless and on the move. . . . Thirty-three people are wearing out their lives and souls like men doomed to imprisonment for life."

By June 1881, the battered, leaky *Jeannette* was being rocked about in the turbulent, icy waters north of the New Siberian Islands. On June 12, the ice finally crushed the ship. The crew dumped three lifeboats and anything else they could save onto an ice floe, and the next morning they began a terrible journey through the Eastern Passage toward the Siberian mainland, which was hundreds of miles away. After two months, one of the boats was lost in a storm; the other two landed separately in the Lena River delta of central Siberia. One of the two surviving parties was able to find a native village, where it remained until its members were rescued. The members of the other party, including De Long, perished on the bleak Siberian tundra.

Apparently unfazed by this tragedy, the Americans continued to probe the Far North. In 1881, the year that Peary joined the navy, the U.S. Army launched the Lady Franklin Bay Expedition. The nominal objective of this expedition was to establish and maintain a scientific outpost on Lady Franklin Bay, at the northern end of Ellesmere Island. But Major Adolphus Washington Greely, the dour but exceptionally courageous Civil War veteran who had been chosen to lead the expedition, had other ideas, and his superiors had given him permission to make an attempt at the Pole if he had the opportunity. If he could not reach the Pole, Greely was determined to at least best the farthest north set by the Nares expedition.

In the summer of 1881, Greely's party of 25 was dropped off by the *Proteus* on the barren north shore of Ellesmere Island, about 600 miles south of the North Pole. There,

Some officers of the Adolphus Greely expedition pose with their dogs outside the hut at Fort Conger, where the expedition spent two grim and dissension-filled winters. Undeniably courageous, Greely tended also to be rigid, pious, and dictatorial; his "indomitable vanity" initially grated on some of his men, who would later have cause to praise his selflessness.

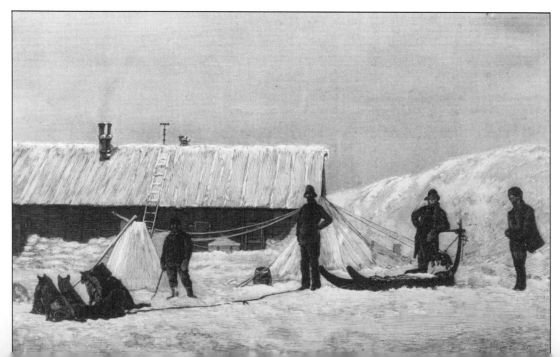

Greely and his men built a small house, which they named Fort Conger. Reconnaissance parties were sent out to survey the area for a possible route to the Pole, while the expedition's Inuit hunters brought in a supply of fresh meat for the winter. Then the men settled in for the long Arctic night. Darkness arrived and stayed, an uninvited guest. Massive polar bears prowled about the camp. Confined to their small cabin, Greely and his men listened to the wind howl and told stories. They whiled away the weeks by playing chess and cards, reading, and publishing a camp newspaper, the *Arctic Moon*. But as the dark weeks became dark months, the inevitable tensions and depressions invaded the little cabin at the top of the world. Lieutenant James Lockwood wrote in his diary that "we often sit silent during the whole day and even a meal fails to elicit anything more than a chance remark or two." One of the dog drivers, an Inuit, ran off into the darkness, intent on suicide. A search party found him wandering about and brought him back to camp.

In April, with the welcome return of the sun, Greely sent out two sledging parties with instructions to go northward as far as they could. The first party was led by the camp physician, Dr. Octave Pavy. The doctor, a cowardly, untrustworthy sort who had spent the winter sowing dissension among the men, did not get far before he was stopped by open water. The second party, led by Lieutenant Lockwood, did better. After crossing Robeson Channel to Greenland, Lockwood's party traveled north up the Greenland coast past Cape Britannia to what is known today as Lockwood Island, bettering the previous farthest north, set by the Nares expedition, by four miles. They planted a small American flag in the ice, and Sergeant David Brainard carved the trademark of his favorite beer across the face of a volcanic cliff. A triumphant Lockwood and his party were back at Fort Conger by June 11, 1882.

Greely and his men spent the summer collecting important meteorological, tidal, and magnetic data. They were all looking forward to the arrival of the relief ship *Neptune*, which was due in August. But August came and went without any sign of the *Neptune*, which had been unable to penetrate thick ice 200 miles south of Fort Conger. Greely's party faced another winter in the high Arctic, with no new supplies and no word from the outside world. They had no choice but to sit it out, which they did,

Starving, freezing, and bordering on collective insanity, Greely and his men await rescue at Camp Clay, the crude shelter they built at Cape Sabine in the winter of 1883. This illustration is misleading in one key aspect: Although the hut did indeed have stone walls (an overturned whaleboat served as the roof), it was only three feet high.

experiencing a winter that was much like the previous one, only worse.

In the spring of 1883, Lockwood, Brainard, and an Inuit dog-team driver named Frederick set out to explore Ellesmere Island. Bathed in sunshine and away from gloomy, claustrophobic Fort Conger for the first time in months, the exhilarated trio sledged across the rugged in-

terior of the island, discovering vast glaciers and petrified forests. Their dogs were exhilarated as well, and they pulled tirelessly and barked joyously. But as the summer weeks went by and the *Neptune* failed to appear once again, the mood back at the camp was quite different. As the days grew shorter and colder, a bad feeling crept over the camp. Food supplies were running low, and for all the men, the prospect of another winter at Fort Conger chilled the soul.

Greely decided to head south. He had been told before the expedition started that if the relief ship could not reach Fort Conger, he should go to Cape Sabine, a small island 240 miles south of Fort Conger at the head of Smith Sound. But as they set out on their journey, Greely and his men had no way of knowing that the relief ship destined for Cape Sabine had been eaten by monstrous pack ice below Smith Sound.

The stranded explorers reached Cape Sabine in October. It was a rocky, windswept, godforsaken place. The Inuit hunters soon determined that there was no game anywhere on the island. The men built a primitive little hut of stones and wood and waited. Night closed in on them, bringing heavy snow. Their food supply dwindled steadily. One of the men, Sergeant Joseph Elison, went out into a howling blizzard to search for a cache of frozen meat that had been left at nearby Ross Bay years earlier by the Nares expedition. He was found eight days later by Brainard and one of the Inuit hunters, frozen into his sleeping bag and in such pain that he begged his friends to kill him. They carried him back to the hut, where it was discovered that his feet and hands were utterly frozen. His fingers and toes turned black and began to drop off. By January he had neither feet nor hands. He attached a spoon to one of his stumps so he could eat his share of the dwindling rations.

Month after dreary, hungry month went by. One by one the men were dying of starvation in their little hut.

Some of them were going insane, reciting endless lists of various foods they would like to have. They stayed in their sleeping bags for days at a time. Greely did his best to keep their morale up, maintaining a semblance of military discipline and often sacrificing his own meager ration of food so another could have a double portion. Nevertheless, as the food ran out, the little band's desperation grew, and one of the men, who was repeatedly caught stealing rations, was taken out and shot on Greely's orders.

On May 16, 1884, Greely wrote in his diary, "Our last regular rations given out today." By June, only 14 men were still alive. They abandoned the hut, which had been flooded during the spring melt, for a small tent. They began to eat lichen, then insects, then their sealskin garments and leather boots. One of them cannibalized the corpse of the man who had been shot for stealing food. And they continued to die. Too weak to remove the dead from the tent, those who still lived let the corpses stiffen in their sleeping bags.

On June 21, 1884, a launch called the *Cub* appeared off the Cape Sabine shoreline. Piloting the *Cub* was Lieutenant J. C. Colwell, who was part of a U.S. Navy expedition sent out to search for any traces of the lost Greely party. Scanning the barren beach, Colwell saw an unbelievable thing—what looked like a very, very old man making his way unsteadily down to the water. Colwell waved; laboriously, the figure waved back. Ashore, the lieutenant confronted a scarecrow of a man who introduced himself as Sergeant Francis Long of the Greely expedition. Long led Colwell to a partially collapsed tent. Colwell took out a knife, cut an opening in the canvas, and looked inside. One of the ghastly, skeletal creatures within looked up with feverish, glittering eyes at the newcomer. "My God," Colwell said. "Greely, is this you?" Greely took a deep breath, and with great effort replied, "Yes. Seven of us left. Here we are. Dying. Like men." Lieutenant Colwell began to weep.

"To die is easy. . . . It is only hard to strive, to endure, to live," wrote Greely at the height of the gruesome winter he and his men spent at Camp Clay in 1883–84. After the expedition was rescued, accusations of cannibalism were leveled at the survivors, but in his memoirs Greely maintained that he knew "of no law, human or divine, which was broken at Sabine."

The Fates and All Hell

A wave of revulsion and horror swept across the United States as the ordeal of the Greely party became known to the public. Politicians and editorialists began calling for a moratorium on Arctic exploration. "Let there be an end to this folly," a *New York Times* headline declared, but Robert Peary harbored no such thoughts. In fact, he intended to go north as soon as possible. The time had come to replace his Arctic dreams with Arctic realities, no matter how grim and cold those realities might be. It was time to take the first step.

In the summer of 1886, Peary took a leave of absence from the navy, borrowed money from his mother, and booked passage on a whaler bound for Godhavn, a small settlement on the Danish island of Disko, near Greenland. There, he befriended the Dane Christian Maigaard, a like-minded Arctic enthusiast. Peary and Maigaard obtained sledges, dogs, and other supplies and eagerly set out onto the Greenland ice cap. The Arctic treated Peary kindly during his first incursion, allowing him to travel inland for 100 miles and to climb the dome-shaped ice cap to an altitude of 7,525 feet above sea level, bettering all previous distance and altitude records for Greenland. By the time he sailed for home, Peary was convinced that he could cross Greenland completely, something that had never been done before. And he was eager to return, for he had been captivated by the Arctic. "There is no bluer, softer,

Independence Day in the Arctic: Peary flies the Stars and Stripes from a cairn at Navy Cliff on July 4, 1892, at the end of the outward leg of his and Astrup's then unparalleled journey across northern Greenland.

fairer, brighter summer sea in all the tropics than this Sea of Baffin and this Bay of Disco," he wrote. "Icebergs fleck the sapphire waters, [and] blue sea, white bergs, brown and red cliffs, and emerald moss and grass-grown slopes, are bathed in brilliant sunshine."

Peary returned home to a considerable amount of publicity. For the first time, the name Peary began to be mentioned in conjunction with the word Arctic. There

was no longer any chance of his being diverted from his polar quest. His confidence, as well as his rapidly expanding ego, had been stoked by his brief Arctic venture. "My last trip has brought my name before the world," he wrote to his mother in February 1887. "My next will give me a standing in the world. . . . I will [by] next winter be one of the foremost in the highest circles of the capital, and make powerful friends with whom I can shape my

Two Greenland Inuits transport their kayaks overland. Peary took this photograph in 1886, on his first Arctic expedition.

future. . . . Remember, mother, I *must* have fame."

But Robert Peary was still a lieutenant in the U.S. Navy, and before he could return to the Arctic he had duties to fulfill. In early 1887 he was put in charge of the entire canal survey project in Nicaragua. Peary wanted to go north, not south, but although it may have seemed like a bothersome circumstance to him at the time, his reassignment to Nicaragua brought about what was perhaps the most fateful—and fortunate—meeting of his life.

Shortly before he departed Washington, D.C., for Nicaragua, Peary, shopping for a good sun helmet to take with him to the jungle, visited B. H. Steinmetz and Sons haberdashery. While he was trying on helmets—apparently it took him a while to find one that was large enough for his outsized head—Peary happened to mention to the owner of the store that he was looking for a valet to accompany him to Central America. The store owner, Sam Steinmetz, happened to have a young black man named Matthew Henson working for him. Steinmetz thought that Henson would be perfect for the job, and he introduced him to Peary.

Peary was immediately impressed by the 21-year-old Henson. Although he was 10 years younger than Peary, Henson had already led the kind of adventurous life that Peary had always craved. Orphaned at the age of eight, Henson had been adopted by a stepmother who beat him regularly and viciously. At the age of 11, Henson ran away and hiked from Washington, D.C., to Baltimore, Maryland, where he wandered around the docks until he met Captain A. Childs of the *Katie Hines*. Henson convinced the captain to take him aboard as a cabin boy, and for the next five years he lived a venturesome, seagoing life.

During their voyages, Childs taught Henson how to read and write, and by the time the young black man returned to Washington, D.C., at the age of 19 he was an accomplished and worldly seaman and traveler. Since then, he had been casting about for new opportunities. As he and

(continued on page 65)

Chilly Scenes of Winter

Lieutenant Samuel Gurney Cresswell of the Royal Navy, who was aboard, painted this portrait of the Investigator, *commanded by Robert McClure, as it made its way east from the Bering Strait through the Beaufort Sea in 1850 as part of the search for Sir John Franklin's lost expedition.*

The Arctic has been the subject of artistic treatment virtually as long as the North Pole has been the object of obsessed explorers. Although few Arctic expeditions made a place for trained artists, even in the 18th and 19th centuries, a time when "scientific" explorers of other regions seldom thought of setting out without a skilled draftsman to compile a visual record of their escapades, a rich legacy of polar art exists nonetheless, for something about the frigid latitudes above the Arctic Circle compelled even the amateur artist to make the attempt to capture their icy essence. The earliest known artistic representation from an Arctic exploration voyage is John White's 1577 drawing of a skirmish between the men of Martin Frobisher's second Northwest Passage expedition and some Greenland Inuits; by the time Robert Peary was making his assaults on the North Pole, of course, the pencil and brush had given way to the camera as the primary means of visual documentation of Arctic exploration. Seen on this and the succeeding pages is a sampler of some of this Arctic art, ranging in level of artistic achievement from the primitive to the exceptionally accomplished, all of it of immense historic significance.

This engraving illustrated the published edition of the journal of Gerrit de Veer, one of only a dozen survivors of the Dutch mariner Willem Barents's third and last attempt to sail the Northeast Passage above Europe and Asia. Barents, who was not among the survivors, set sail on his final voyage in 1596.

Trapping foxes and hunting polar bears: This illustration from de Veer's journal, which was published in 1599, shows how the men of the Barents expedition survived the winter of "great cold, poverty, misery, and grief" they endured on Novaya Zemlya, an archipelago in the Barents Sea.

The men of the Barents expedition haul driftwood to be used in building their winter shelter on Novaya Zemlya.

An interior view of the shelter of the cabin on Novaya Zemlya reveals a sick man dozing by the fire, sleeping cubicles against the back wall, and a bathing apparatus made from a wine cask. The clock hanging high on the right-hand wall soon stopped chiming because of the cold.

Ross himself was an enthusiastic sketcher and painter of Arctic scenes. He did this drawing of an Inuit settlement in the course of his second Arctic voyage, which lasted from 1829 to 1833. He wrote that the Inuits "were delighted with the identity of the representation when the sketch was finished, each recognizing his own house."

John Sacheuse, an Inuit employed by the Royal Navy as an interpreter, drew this picture of the first encounter between the officers of John Ross's 1819 Arctic expedition and the Inuits of Etah, on the coast of Greenland. Ross's voyage was the first European or American Arctic expedition of the 19th century.

In this Ross sketch of September 1819, gunshots from one of Ross's ships— either the Isabella or the Alexander—send a polar bear diving for the water from the ice floe where it had been basking.

61

William Bradford, of the whaling town of New Bedford, Massachusetts, was among the few professional artists of his day to visit the Arctic. This painting, entitled Ice Dwellers Watching the Invaders, *was the product of his 1869 voyage to Melville Bay, the eighth voyage he had made to the Far North in order "to study Nature under the terrible aspects of the Frigid Zone."*

Ross's depiction of an arctic fox.
During the search for Franklin's lost
expedition, the British tried to use
arctic foxes as couriers by tying
messages for the missing explorer
to the animals' tails.

(continued from page 56)

Peary sized up one another in the Washington haber-dashery, something about the navy man's manner suggested to Henson that Peary was destined to do something extraordinary. Peary, for his part, liked Henson's self-confidence and intelligence. He offered the job of valet to Henson, who accepted. Thus began a remarkable relationship and, for Henson, a remarkable career. Matt Henson would become indispensable to Peary; he would also become a great Arctic explorer in his own right, although his accomplishments would be overshadowed by Peary's.

Peary, with Henson in tow, returned to Nicaragua in late 1887. He was back in Washington by August 1888, having performed brilliantly as a field leader during the canal survey. On August 11, Peary married Josephine Diebitsch, after which he and his new bride (and his mother as well) vacationed in Sea Bright, New Jersey. But the honeymoon was soon over, interrupted by the actions of Fridtjof Nansen, a man neither Peary nor his wife had ever met. Nansen, a brilliant Norwegian explorer, had succeeded in crossing the Greenland ice cap that summer, a feat that Peary had hoped to accomplish himself. Upstaged by the Norwegian, Peary fumed. Although he had only been to the Arctic once, Peary already believed that it was rightfully "his." This competitive attitude would intensify over the years to one of jealousy and paranoia.

By the summer of 1891, Peary had wrangled another leave from the navy and was ready to return to the Arctic. This time, he would go as the leader of a full-scale expedition. He had raised $10,000 from various contributors—including the American Geographical Society, the Brooklyn Institute, and the Philadelphia Academy of Natural Sciences—and had hired a ship to take his fully outfitted party north. Sailing with him aboard the *Kite* were ornithologist Langdon Gibson, geologist John M. Verhoeff, Norwegian skier Eivind Astrup, Matthew Henson, the young New York physician Dr. Frederick A. Cook, and Peary's wife, Josephine.

Peary and his party at McCormick Bay in 1891. Josephine Peary stands next to her husband; seated from left to right are Dr. Frederick Cook, Matthew Henson, Eivind Astrup, John Verhoeff, and Langdon Gibson.

The voyage was an unlucky one for Peary; his leg was broken by the *Kite*'s iron tiller. When the ship reached its destination at McCormick Bay, high on Greenland's west coast, Peary—to his embarrassment—was carried ashore strapped to a wooden board. This was hardly the entry of a Cortés, but Peary was dutifully cared for by Dr. Cook and his wife, and soon he was mobile once again.

The company spent the summer and fall organizing their base camp, which was located about 80 miles from the dread Cape Sabine. They built a small house atop a cliff overlooking the bay, which Peary named Red Cliff House because of the reddish lichen that covered the face of the promontory. Peary sent out sledging parties to cache supplies along the northward route he intended to take to the ice cap in the spring.

The long Arctic night settled in over McCormick Bay. Peary spent most of the time hunched over a table in the little cabin, plotting and planning by candlelight. He drew up plans for new sledges and boats that would be lighter but stronger than the customary models. He estimated the absolute minimum amount of men and supplies that would be necessary to cross the ice cap. Unlike the British, who liked to send whole armies of men into the Arctic, as if they could subdue it by sheer force of numbers, Peary wanted to keep his parties as small, unencumbered, and mobile as possible.

And, wisely taking a page from Charles Hall's Arctic canon, Peary studied the Inuit. Inuit hunters began visiting the camp in the early winter, and Peary and the other members of the expedition encouraged them to bring their families and stay. The friendly, social Inuit set up camp near Red Cliff House and began to barter and interact daily with Peary's party. Peary questioned these Arctic natives extensively about their methods of hunting, traveling, and keeping warm. Soon the Inuit men were instructing Peary and his men on how to hunt musk-oxen and handle a dog team, and the Inuit women were sewing sealskin clothing for the expedition. Henson and the Inuit took a special liking to one another, forming bonds that

Peary took this photo of Greenland Inuits in their kayaks. According to Peary, the "distinctive feature" of his plan to reach the North Pole was the "adoption of Eskimo methods and costumes." This was one of the most significant facets of the "American method" of polar exploration, although Peary was not the first of his countrymen to learn and use native survival techniques.

would last for decades. Henson adapted to their ways quite readily, and by springtime, he was expert at building igloos, hunting Arctic game, and driving a dog team.

Finally, the first sign of spring began to glimmer on the horizon. On May 3, 1892, with Astrup, Cook, and Gibson (Henson remained at camp with a frostbitten heel), Peary started northward, intending to cross Greenland's ice cap to its far northeast corner, which was as yet unexplored. From there, he hoped to find a route to the Pole or at least to determine whether or not Greenland was an island. After traveling 130 miles to the source of the Humboldt Glacier, Peary, according to plan, sent Cook and Gibson back to camp. Then, on April 30, Peary and Astrup set out on a journey that was to instantly propel Peary into the ranks of the most accomplished Arctic explorers.

Driving 13 dogs before them, clothed in Inuit sealskin and blocking the new sunlight with smoked glasses, the two men moved swiftly across the brilliant ice cap, gaining altitude and degrees of latitude as they went. Five hundred miles and six weeks later, with their food supplies gone and their dogs exhausted, they reached the northeastern edge of the ice cap at what is known today as Kennedy Bay. There, the two men were greeted by a vision of stunning, terrible beauty. "A few steps more," Peary wrote, "and the rocky plateau on which we stood dropped in a giant iron wall that would grace the Inferno, 3,800 feet to the level of the bay below us. We stood upon the northeast coast of Greenland and, looking far over the surface of a mighty glacier on our right and through the broad mouth of the bay, we saw stretching away to the horizon the great ice-fields of the Arctic Ocean."

Peary and Astrup would go no farther. If they were going to make it back to camp before winter arrived, they would have to start immediately. They had eaten all their food; for the return journey they needed enough not only to feed themselves but the ravenous dogs as well. They set out on a musk-oxen hunt. Their exhilaration had worn

off; now they were just two profoundly isolated men trapped without food on the top of the world. The hunt was quiet and desperate, and for the first time Peary truly understood the harsh, pitiless nature of the Arctic. No food had ever tasted as good as the fresh and bloodily raw musk-oxen meat he shared with Astrup and the dogs after their hunt had succeeded. And no homecoming was ever as sweet as the one he experienced at Red Cliff House in late August, when he and Astrup completed their 500-mile homeward trek. The Arctic had not let the party escape unscathed, however. John Verhoeff, the young geologist, had never returned to camp from an exploratory excursion, and thus the *Kite* sailed for home with one less passenger.

Peary returned to the United States a man obsessed. More than ever before, he believed that the North Pole was his destiny. He immediately began making plans for

A supply cache on what Peary hoped would prove to be the "imperial highway" to the Pole. Peary and his men built igloos to sleep in as well as to use as storehouses for supplies.

Marie Ahnighito Peary was born at Anniversary Lodge, where this picture was taken, on September 12, 1893. Peary took this photo as a ray of sunlight shone into his room; his daughter "reached for the golden bar as other children reach for a beautiful toy." During his years in the Arctic, Peary also fathered two sons by a young Inuit woman.

his next expedition with the same tireless energy that had propelled him across the Greenland ice cap. In order to raise money, he went out on the lecture circuit, accompanied by an unhappy Henson and an even more unhappy team of huskies. Charging $2,000 per lecture, Peary made 165 appearances in 103 days. The lectures were a sensation. Peary and Henson, along with the dogs, would appear onstage in full Arctic regalia. Peary would then spin Arctic yarns for an hour or two, and the circus would move on to the next town. With the funds from this tour and private contributions, Peary raised enough money to hire another ship and outfit another expedition.

In June 1893, with Henson, Astrup, a pregnant Josephine, and nine new volunteers, Peary sailed for Greenland once again. (It seems that the U.S. Navy had given up on trying to keep Peary home.) His ship, the *Falcon*, took him and his men up the Greenland coast past McCormick Bay to Bowdoin Bay, where Peary set up a new camp, which he named Anniversary Lodge. From there, he intended to cross the ice cap once again, continue his reconnaissance of northwest Greenland, and, if possible, make a run from Independence Bay to the Pole.

On September 12, the imperturbable Josephine gave birth to the Pearys' first child. They named her Marie Ahnighito Peary—Ahnighito is Inuit for "Snow Baby." Inuits came from far and wide to marvel at the child's pale skin and sky-blue eyes. But soon after the birth of the snow baby, things began to go wrong. On Halloween, 1893, a gigantic iceberg broke off the face of neighboring Bowdoin Glacier and crashed into the sea, causing, in Peary's words, "a roaring cataract of water" to boil up out of the bay and swamp the camp, smashing equipment and carrying off supplies when it receded. Peary, who was away from camp at the time, roared himself when he heard the news. "The fates and all hell are against me!" he cried.

If the fates and all hell were not against Peary during his third Greenland excursion, the Arctic certainly was.

His March 1894 attempt to cross "his" ice cap again was met with the kind of Arctic fury he had yet to experience. Eight days out of Anniversary Lodge, he and his eight companions were stopped in their tracks by a savage storm. Forty-mile-per-hour winds and temperatures that dropped to 60 degrees below zero drove them back to camp.

In August, when the *Falcon* returned to take the party home, Peary informed his wife that he would stay at Anniversary Lodge for another year. He had spent the summer brooding over his spring failure, and he was determined to stay at Bowdoin Bay until he had another chance to cross the ice cap and make an assault on the Pole. In making this decision, Peary had stepped over the line that separates ordinary men from the possessed.

In April 1895, accompanied by Hugh Lee and the faithful Henson—the only two members of the expedition who had elected to stay with him—as well as 6 Inuits and 60 dogs, Peary set out across the "Great Ice" again. The party made good progress initially, but the going was rough and the men were worn down steadily. One by one the Inuits turned back and the dogs expired. By the time Peary, Henson, and Lee reached Independence Bay, only 11 dogs remained and the rations were dangerously low. Once again, Peary had failed to reach the Arctic Ocean, and once again he found himself engaged in a desperate hunt for musk-oxen. Fortunately, the stalwart Henson, who had already developed into a prodigious Arctic hunter, was equal to the task. But even with the meat from seven musk-oxen and the dead dogs to fortify them, the journey back to Anniversary Lodge almost killed the three men. They reached Bowdoin Bay in a deplorable state on June 25. Only one dog, Panikpah, was left. As he descended from the ice, Panikpah could not struggle over the rocks and lay down at a distance from the lodge to rest. Peary crawled into the lodge and collapsed, too tired to eat. When Panikpah finally came in, Peary roused himself and ate, but not before he fed the dog.

Panikpah was the sole canine survivor of Peary's 1895 trek with Henson and Hugh Lee. For weeks after their return to Anniversary Lodge, Panikpah, who had nearly died of hunger and exhaustion, hoarded away every bone and piece of meat he could get his paws on

The Great Adventure of the Ice

When Robert Peary returned from Greenland to the United States in 1895, he was greeted with a letter from his mother in which she said, among other things, "If you have not accomplished all you had hoped to, do not be disheartened; take a cheerful view of your future. *Many have failed.*"

This was the last thing Peary wanted to hear. It was almost as if his mother were mocking him. Although the three giant meteorites and the six live Inuits he brought back with him from the Arctic proved to be great sources of income and publicity and he was now being lauded by the press and the most influential scientific societies as a great Arctic explorer and perhaps the greatest of all the Americans to challenge the Arctic, Peary considered himself to be just one of the "many" who had failed, for he had not reached the Pole. He seethed with his failure. There was nothing to do but return to the Arctic as soon as he could raise enough money to finance another expedition. Once again he began the tedious business of soliciting contributions and petitioning for another extended leave from the navy. Peary felt a new sense of urgency—he was almost 40 now. And, to his dismay, the only other explorer he truly feared—Fridtjof Nansen, the man who had ruined Peary's honeymoon—was at large in the Arctic once more.

Fridtjof Nansen's Arctic explorations made him Norway's greatest hero. Nansen emphasized meticulous preparation, small, carefully trained parties, and the use of skis—what came to be the fundamental tenets of the so-called Norwegian school of exploration. After his exploring days, he helped engineer Norway's independence from Sweden, served as a diplomat, and eventually won the Nobel Peace Prize for his work with World War I refugees.

If Robert Peary saw the Arctic as his archenemy, Fridtjof Nansen viewed it as his ally and his muse. "I found in the [Arctic] the great adventure of the ice, deep and pure as infinity, the silent starry night, the depths of Nature herself, the fullness of the mystery of life, the eternal round of the universe and its eternal death." Thus did Nansen write of the Arctic, a place that did not intimidate or challenge or enrage him but rather inspired him.

Fridtjof Nansen, along with Otto Sverdrup, Baron A. E. Nordenskiöld, and Roald Amundsen (who would eventually navigate the Northwest Passage and conquer the South Pole), was one of a new group of Scandinavian explorers that came to the Arctic regions in the final decade of the 19th century—a group of men who would permanently banish the idea of British and American supremacy at the top (or bottom) of the world. These Norsemen, and Nansen in particular, were a breed apart, well equipped both physically and psychologically for Arctic exploration. Accustomed to the rigors of the Far North and the high Arctic, they were natural skiers, hunters, and dog-sled handlers. Stolid but not stubborn, fearless but never foolhardy, relentless but never impatient, they approached the Arctic with respect but also with the Viking's innate, indomitable self-confidence. And, perhaps most importantly, they seemed impervious to the mental and emotional horrors that bedeviled so many British and American Arctic explorers.

Blond, six feet tall, and powerfully built, Nansen looked like a Viking warrior but was in fact a serious scientist who was well versed in zoology, oceanography, mathematics, and astronomy. Nansen had the calculating mind of a scientist but the heart of a poet-adventurer, and the plan he announced to the public in 1892—a scheme that Nansen believed might just take him to the North Pole—was equal parts science and poetry. And, like all great plans and strategies, it was sublimely simple and direct. He proposed, to the astonishment of his fellow Arctic enthusiasts the world over, to offer himself up to the Arctic Ocean as a piece of human driftwood. Why fight the great, perilous ice pack? Nansen asked. If you instead befriend it and enlist its aid, it might carry you all the way to the Pole! In short, Nansen proposed to deliberately take a ship into the teeth of the ice pack off the coast of Siberia and then to let the steadily westward drifting pack carry him across the Arctic Ocean to within striking distance of the Pole.

"Balderdash!" the experts thundered. "Preposterous!" "Madness!" "Quite unthinkable!" First of all, they pointed out to Nansen, it had never been proved that there was a steady east-to-west current across the Arctic Ocean. And secondly, Nansen would never live to find out, for the ice would devour his ship just as it had devoured all the others.

Fridtjof Nansen thought not. Had not wreckage from the doomed *Jeannette*, crushed by the ice in Siberian waters back in 1881, washed up on the shores of Greenland? Had not sediment from Siberian rivers and wood from Siberian trees been found in the waters off Greenland's east coast? Did this not prove the existence of a westerly transpolar current?

Perhaps, the doubters allowed. Perhaps there was a current. But what about the ship? The ice had destroyed even the largest and most powerful of the British navy's vessels. No ship could survive the ceaseless grinding and hammering of the Arctic ice for an indefinite period. If there was a transpolar current, it would be a very slow one. It might take years for Nansen to drift across the Arctic Ocean, and a ship could withstand the pounding for only so long.

Nansen's answer to these questions was the *Fram* (Forward)—the most famous vessel in the history of Arctic (and Antarctic) exploration. Nansen designed the *Fram* himself, and it was custom built by Colin Archer, a masterful Scottish shipwright then living in Norway, for surviving the ice pack. It was small—the *Fram* would carry a crew of but 13—compared to most previous Arctic vessels

(continued on page 78)

Peary and the Inuit

P eary's success as an Arctic explorer was based in large part on his adaptation of traditional Inuit methods of travel and survival in a frigid environment, an innovation for which he was justly praised. From the Inuit, he learned how to build igloos, drive dog teams, and wear and design fur clothing that kept the body warm, dry, and comfortable. That kind of knowledge was available to all who visited the Arctic, but only Peary demonstrated the foresight to make use of it to such an extent. British explorers, for example, were notably and haughtily resistant to using native survival methods, to their detriment and sometimes their death. (It is significant to note that the first man to reach the South Pole, the estimable Norwegian explorer Roald Amundsen in 1912, had also made a thorough study of Inuit lifeways and relied on native survival methods.)

Yet there is a troublesome element of Peary's relationship with the Inuit, one that smacks of calculating, heedless exploitation. "Of what use are Eskimos to the world?" he wrote once. "They are too far removed to be of any value for commercial enterprises; and furthermore they lack ambition. They have no literature, nor, properly speaking, any art. They value life only as does a fox, or a bear, purely by instinct. But let us not forget that these people, trustworthy and hardy, will yet prove their value to mankind. With their help, the world shall discover the Pole." With their help, *I* shall discover the Pole, he might have more honestly written.

Having failed on his 1893–95 expedition to make either any significant headway toward the Pole or important geographical discoveries, Peary brought back with him from Greenland three meteorites—one the largest then known—and sold them to the American Museum of Natural History in New York City for the princely sum of $40,000. The knowledge that in so doing he had deprived the Inuit on Greenland of their only source of metal, the means that had enabled, in his own words, "an entire aboriginal tribe . . . to rise from the stone to the iron age," did not greatly trouble him. He justified his action by reasoning that he had provided the Inuit with enough modern tools and equipment to render the meteorites superfluous.

On board the same ship that carried the great meteorite southward were six Inuit men and, in "five big barrels," the jumbled bones of several dead Inuit whose graves Peary had robbed. The bones were sold to the Museum of Natural History along with the meteorites, and the six living specimens were housed in the museum's damp basement. Within a short time, four of the six, including "Nooktah, my faithful hunter and dog driver" and "Kessuh, or the Smiler," as Peary referred to two of them in his book *Northward Over the Great Ice*, contracted influenza and tuberculosis and died. Their remains were soon put on exhibit in the museum.

Their fate did not distress Peary, although it did cause him some embarrassment. GIVE ME MY FATHER'S BODY, a New York *World* headline demanded on January 6, 1907. Minik, the young son of Qisuk, one of the dead Inuits, had learned that the burial of his father on the museum grounds that he had witnessed nine years earlier was a sham concocted to prevent him from learning that his father's corpse had been dissected and the bones bleached, reassembled, and mounted. Qisuk's skeleton was now an exhibit behind glass in one of the Museum of Natural History's galleries. When Peary washed his hands of the scandal and the museum refused to return the bones for a proper burial, an embittered Minik returned to Greenland, convinced that Peary and his countrymen were a "race of scientific criminals."

Members of the Peary expedition pose with some Inuits along the coast of Greenland in 1908. Matthew Henson is just left of center; to an extent much greater than Peary, Henson mastered the Inuit language and came to truly know and appreciate their way of life.

One of the Fram's *crew takes an ocean sounding. The windmill-like device on the deck was used to power a generator in order to provide electricity. Greely, who called it an "illogical scheme of self-destruction," was just one of many supposed Arctic experts who derided Nansen's plans for the polar drift.*

(continued from page 75)

and therefore more maneuverable and able to slip through leads and cracks in the ice that would entrap a larger ship. It had a specially reinforced hull. Most important was the shape of the hull, which was rounded like an old bathtub. Nansen reasoned—correctly, as it turned out—that when the ice closed in on the rounded hull, the *Fram* would not be caught and crushed in a frigid vice but would instead be squeezed upward until it rode atop, rather than within, the drifting ice. In Nansen's own words, the *Fram* would "slip like an eel out of the embraces of the ice." But the skeptics were unconvinced.

On June 24, 1893, the *Fram* steamed out of Norway's Christiania Harbor with Nansen, the redoubtable Captain Otto Sverdrup, 11 other carefully chosen Norwegians, and 3 dozen dogs aboard. After sailing around the north coast of Europe to Yugor Strait, then past Asia through the Kara Sea and around Cape Chelyuskin, Sverdrup drove the powerful little *Fram* into the ice pack north of the New

Siberian Islands—the very ice that had crushed the *Jeannette*. By September 25, the *Fram* was solidly frozen into the pack. The long westward drift had begun.

No previous Arctic expedition had ever proceeded so smoothly. Had Nansen's critics known how smoothly, they would have been rendered speechless. Once their ship was firmly frozen in, the *Fram*'s crew hauled in the rudder, dismantled, oiled, and stored the engine, and settled in for the winter. They turned the little *Fram* into a miniature Norwegian village square, complete with workshops for a joiner, a mechanic, a blacksmith, a tinsmith, a shoemaker, and a sailmaker, not to mention a printing press, where a weekly journal, *Framjaa*, was printed. "There was nothing," Nansen wrote, "from the most delicate instrument down to wooden shoes and axe-handles that could not be made on board the *Fram*." The crew even set up a windmill to drive an electricity-producing dynamo that provided electric light for the ship. What a strange sight the self-sufficient little vessel must have made out on the vast ice pack, glowing cheerily in the Arctic gloom.

And as Nansen had expected, the *Fram* handled the ice with ease, popping up above it like a wet bar of soap whenever the pressure built up. "All at once in the afternoon," wrote Nansen of the first test of the *Fram*'s special hull, "as we were sitting idly chatting, a deafening noise began and the whole ship shook . . . . Everyone rushed on deck to look . . . . On pushed the ice, but down under us it had to go, and we were slowly lifted up." Eventually, the men grew so confident in the little ship's ability to ride with the ice that they no longer bothered to go out on deck when the intense grinding of the floes started up.

And so Nansen's epic drift continued. The journey was long and monotonous—30 months over an erratic 400-mile course across the top of the world. The men remained healthy, well fed, and in good spirits. They spent their time taking care of the dogs and reading books from the

Fram's substantial library. The detailed scientific chores—astronomical observations every other day; magnetic readings and ocean soundings periodically—helped to relieve the tedium, but by late 1894 Nansen was so bored that he was praying for a blizzard. By January 1895, Nansen had realized that the drifting ice would carry him no farther north, which left the *Fram* more than 400 miles south of the Pole. His time of boredom was over—he began making plans for a dash across the ice.

Fridtjof Nansen's attempt to reach the North Pole from the *Fram* is still regarded as one of the most audacious acts in the history of exploration. Some explorers, including Peary, regarded it as an almost suicidal attempt, for once Nansen left his faithful *Fram* behind, it would drift inexorably away, and Nansen would have to find his way back to land himself, with only his dogsled, kayak, and two legs to carry him. But Nansen himself approached the journey with his usual mixture of confidence, enthusiasm, and analytic detachment. He knew it was a gamble, but he felt that the odds were in his favor.

On March 14, Nansen and Lieutenant Frederic Hjalmar Johansen, "a plucky fellow who never gives in," bid a heartfelt farewell to their companions and their floating home and set off across the ice. They would travel on skis

This illustration of the men of the Fram *at dinner appeared in* Farthest North, *Nansen's published account of his Arctic explorations. Nansen (standing at left) believed that Norwegians were uniquely suited to withstand the intense psychological pressures of the Arctic winter, a theory that his* Fram *expedition seemed to verify.*

with 3 light sledges, 28 dogs, 3 kayaks, and food for 100 days. They moved quickly at first, gliding easily across flat, smooth ice. Even these two stoic Norwegians were awed by the immense, unearthly desert of ice as it was illuminated by the flickering, rippling aurora borealis. After two weeks, the flat ice gave way to a jumbled "chaos of ice blocks," and they were forced to pick their way slowly over and around pressure ridges and boulders of ice. And as they toiled northward, the drifting ice carried them southward. The dogs began to drop from exhaustion. The animals would lay panting weakly on the ice; sometimes a dog might revive, and sometimes it might rest its head on its forepaws and die. Still, the little expedition pushed northward. By April 8, the two courageous Norwegians had reached 86 degrees north latitude, 160 miles farther north than any man had ever gone. But they were still more than 200 miles short of the Pole. Food was running low, and the ice behind them was beginning to break up with the spring thaw. Reluctantly, Nansen called a halt

Nansen (second from left) prepares to set out from the Fram *on March 14, 1895, with Hjalmar Johansen (fourth from right) to make his ski-and-sledge assault on the Pole. The prospect of leaving the* Fram, *Nansen wrote, left him overcome with a "wave of sadness," for it was "like bidding farewell to a dear friend."*

At the Poles, Hjalmar Johansen
was equal to any challenge, but
everyday life posed greater
obstacles for him. Back in
Norway following the Fram
expedition, Johansen sank into
alcoholism. A position with
Roald Amundsen's 1910 South
Pole expedition, secured for him
by Nansen, offered a chance at
rehabilitation, but Johansen was
deeply hurt that he was not
subsequently chosen for the polar
party itself. Further drinking,
increasing despondency, and
suicide followed.

to the march; to go any farther would have indeed been
suicidal.

Now Nansen and Johansen were faced with the task of
reaching the nearest land—a group of small islands 400
miles to the southwest, in the Barents Sea at the southern
edge of the ice pack. They began trudging doggedly southward. The once-solid ice was now constantly shifting,
churning, and bubbling. As spring turned to summer, the
sun lingered in the sky longer every day and then simply
circled the horizon, never setting. The two men began to
hate the omnipresent orb that set this icy, watery world
aglimmer with a harsh, blinding brightness, and they
yearned for the cool, constant darkness of the Arctic winter.

As the ice continued to break up around them, Nansen
and Johansen were forced to take to the kayaks more frequently. They ran out of food in July and began eating
their dogs one by one. At the end of the month, they
barely avoided becoming a meal themselves when they
were stalked by a hungry polar bear. Soon after they es-
caped the bear, they reached the edge of the ice; before
them was the open water of the Barents Sea. They killed
the rest of the dogs, stored the meat in their kayaks, and
then, tying the kayaks together and fashioning a sail, took
to the water. Almost a month later, they sighted one of
the northern islands of Franz Josef Land. For the first time
in more than three years, Nansen and Johansen felt solid
earth beneath their feet.

Winter was closing in again. The little island was un-
inhabited, but there was plenty of game, and Nansen and
Johansen had no trouble putting in a store of walrus and
polar bear meat. They dug a small hole in the ice, lined
and covered it with walrus and bear skins, and as the Arctic
night came down again they crawled contentedly into their
den and prepared to sleep through the winter like two hiber-
nating bears. In May 1896 they emerged blinking from their
cave and headed south again. By June they had reached
one of the southernmost islands of Franz Josef Land.

Early on the morning of June 17, Nansen heard the sound of dogs barking and went to investigate. Walking toward him was a man in a checkered suit, high rubber boots, and a bowler. Nansen was astonished and thought he must be hallucinating. The man in the suit was just as astonished, for the figure that approached him looked like some wild, hairy, yeti-like creature. The two strangers confronted one another. Being an Englishman, the man in the checkered suit politely doffed his hat. He was amazed when the yeti responded by bowing courteously. The Englishman, an explorer named Frederick Jackson, saw a pair of calm, lucid blue eyes regarding him from amid the filthy, matted hair and beard. Suddenly, it dawned on him. "By Jove!" he exclaimed. "Aren't you Nansen?" Nansen smiled. "By Jove!" Jackson exclaimed again, for Fridtjof Nansen had long since been given up for dead. "By Jove!"

The very top of the world was the great geographical prize aspired to by Nansen and Peary.

I Will Stake My Life on the Throw

Fridtjof Nansen's seemingly miraculous return from the dead made him nothing less than a saint in his homeland and a hero internationally, and admiration for him continued to grow as the facts of his amazing odyssey became known to the public. Peary, for his part, breathed a sigh of relief that Nansen had not reached the Pole and returned to the frenzy of preparation in which he had been engaged.

For his next expedition, Peary had decided to utilize a new strategy. Like Nansen, he had commissioned the design of a specially customized Arctic vessel. This ship, the *Windward*, reflected Peary's personal approach to polar exploration just as the *Fram* reflected Nansen's. Nansen's vessel had been designed to work *with* the Arctic environment; Peary's *Windward* was designed to overpower the ice. The *Windward* was an armored steam yacht overhauled to carry extremely powerful state-of-the-art engines. With this vessel, Peary intended to bully his way up through Smith Sound, Kane Basin, and Kennedy and Robeson channels to the northernmost tip of Greenland or Ellesmere Island, where he would set up a permanent base camp.

Peary was approaching this expedition as if it were his last. He made it clear to his family, friends, and sponsors that this time he intended to stay in the Arctic until he reached the Pole and that if he could not return with his goal accomplished he would not return at all. "The

Peary's dog team crosses a huge crevasse on the surface of a glacier. Such crevasses were a commonplace hazard of Arctic travel.

chances," Peary wrote, "which an expedition of one season now and another a dozen or more years later have of striking a favorable season [for an assault on the Pole] are small. . . . The only way is to lie in wait at some favorable point and watch season after season, ready to take advantage of a favorable one, and believe me, there will come that season when the fortunate man waiting on the verge of the unknown region can, when the moment arrives, shoot forward to the Pole like a ball from a cannon. . . . To the patient waiter and the persistent devil all things come round in time, and I will be both. I will stake my life on the throw of that favorable season . . . and live there on the shore of the Northern ocean till the secret is wrested from the ice or I leave my life."

In order to place himself "on the shore of the Northern ocean," Peary needed two things—money and an extended leave from the navy. By this time, Peary had become a master of self-promotion, and with the help of a group of powerful businessmen and politicians who wanted to see the American flag placed on the Pole first, by 1898 he had succeeded in obtaining financing and a five-year leave. And yet the fates still seemed to be against him: A shipbuilders strike in England delayed the installation of the *Windward*'s all-important new engines. And, to Peary's dismay, word was out that the Norwegians were planning to return to the Arctic. Captain Otto Sverdrup had announced that he would be piloting the *Fram* (which, like Nansen, had emerged from its previous Arctic odyssey in splendid shape) into the Smith Sound–Kane Basin area. Although Sverdrup had asserted that he would not try for the Pole but would instead be engaging in scientific research, Peary was convinced that the Norwegians were planning to ruin his life by taking a shot at the Pole.

Although the *Windward*'s new engines were not yet ready, Peary could wait no longer, and in the spring of 1898 he steamed north in a ship that was nowhere near as powerful as the one he had envisioned. It was stopped

dead by the ice in Kane Basin that December, 250 miles
south of Fort Conger, Peary's goal. Only 40 miles away
was the *Fram*, locked into the same ice. The presence of
the rival ship ate away at Peary, and he spent most of his
time pacing the iced-over deck of his own ship, muttering
to himself about treacherous Norwegians. The result of
all this was the near-fatal march to Fort Conger made by
Peary, Henson, Dr. Dedrick, and four Inuit men in late
January 1899.

Thus it was that Peary found himself languishing in the
cabin at Fort Conger, a place still haunted by the despair
and horror of the Greely expedition. Indeed, the remains
of the Greely party's final meal before their march to Cape
Sabine were still laid out on the table, the biscuits and
coffee perfectly preserved by the Arctic cold after almost
15 years. In excruciating pain from his ravaged feet, trapped in the ghostly cabin while the high-Arctic winter raged
outside, Peary seemed to sink into a depression, prostrate
on a cot in a darkened corner outside the meager circle
of light cast by the oil lamps on the table. Later, Peary
would describe those weeks as "black" and "interminable,"
and indeed, this was the low point of all his years in the
Arctic. With food running out and its commander physically and emotionally immobilized, the expedition was
in danger of perishing. Only the efforts of Matt Henson,
who ventured out into the fierce Arctic night and engaged
in a Herculean hunt for musk-oxen—a hunt that acquired
such legendary status among the Inuit that it is still re-
counted in reverent tones by them today—saved the party
from disaster.

When the first splash of spring light appeared on the
horizon, Henson, the doctor, and the Inuit men lashed
Peary to a sledge and began the journey back to the *Windward*, a trip that was as grueling as the previous one. Peary
endured subzero temperatures and the bumping and grinding of the sledge in silence. Back aboard the ship, he
endured further surgery on his feet; because of a limited

The Inuit regarded Matthew Henson with great affection. They called him Miy Paluk, which meant "my little Matthew" in their language, and he was always welcome in their villages. Many years after Henson left the Arctic, the Inuit still told stories of his courageous feats.

supply of anesthetic, he regained consciousness before the operation was finished.

While Peary lay recovering from the surgery in his cabin during the weeks that followed, Henson and the other members of the expedition concluded that they would be leaving the Arctic as soon as the weather permitted. Certainly, they reasoned, Peary was finished. But in March, Peary emerged on crutches from his cabin and informed them that they would be returning to Fort Conger. With Peary once again strapped to a sledge like so much luggage, bellowing orders and encouragements to his men, the explorers made a return march to Fort Conger. They reached that grim outpost in May, but their attempts to cross Robeson Channel to Greenland were unsuccessful. Forced to retreat to the *Windward* once again, Peary had Greely's cabin at Fort Conger destroyed before he departed, as if the memories it housed had jinxed his own efforts.

Peary was back at Fort Conger by March 1900. Henson and some Inuit hunters had spent the previous winter there building new cabins and hunting musk-oxen, so there were comfortable quarters and an ample supply of food waiting for Peary when he arrived. In May, Peary, Henson, and an Inuit departed behind 3 sledges and 16 dogs for the north coast of Greenland. They crossed the frozen Robeson Channel successfully and headed northward up the Greenland coastline. On May 8, they reached the farthest north set by Lockwood and Brainard of the Greely expedition 18 years before. Five days later they were at the northernmost tip of Greenland. For the first time, Peary ventured out onto the frozen Arctic Ocean, the final obstacle between himself and the realization of his lifelong dream. But within a matter of days the ice pack had beaten him back, and the party started the long retreat to Fort

Peary's determination to reach the North Pole exceeded that of any other polar explorer. "[I will] live there on the shore of the northern ocean till the secret is wrested from the ice or I leave my life," he vowed before undertaking his 1898 expedition.

Conger. There, Peary settled in for yet another winter. In late August, a relief ship arrived. Dr. Frederick Cook, who had accompanied Peary on one of his first Greenland expeditions, was aboard. He examined Peary and told him that his days as an Arctic traveler were over. Peary told him to go away and began planning for a new assault on the Pole in the spring.

In March 1902, Peary, Henson, and seven Inuits sledged up Robeson Channel to Cape Hecla, one of the northernmost points on Ellesmere Island. From there they set out across the ice pack, heading due north for the pole. By April 21 they had reached 84 degrees north latitude— a new farthest north for Peary—but the Pole was still 395 miles away. Exhausted, frozen, and sick in mind and body, Peary called a halt to the march. The party struggled back to Fort Conger, and by mid-August a disconsolate Peary was homeward bound aboard the *Windward*. "The game is off. My dream of sixteen years is over. . . . I have made a good fight, but I cannot accomplish the impossible," a seemingly beaten Peary wrote in his journal. But during the voyage, Peary and Henson were told that an Italian expedition had set a new farthest north, breaking the record set by Nansen. "Next time I'll smash that all to bits!" snarled Peary. *"Next time?"* thought Henson.

"My dear, dear Father: Of course I know the [news]papers are not always right, but I read that the Peary Arctic Club are trying to get [you] to go north again. I think it is a dog's shame and wish every member of the Club were dead then you would not have to go in the first place. I know you will do what pleases Mother and me and that is to stay with us at home. I have been looking at your pictures it seems ten years and I am sick of looking at them. I want to see my father. I don't want people to think me an orphan. Please think this over. Your loving Marie."

This was nine-year-old Marie Peary's reaction to learning that Peary's supporters—the Peary Arctic Club—were planning another expedition for her father. Peary's wife's feelings were no different; Josephine felt that the Arctic had literally stolen her husband away from her, and she pleaded with the president of the Peary Arctic Club to "let me keep my old man at home." Yet Peary was as unmoved by their pleas as the Arctic ice itself might have been, and by 1903 the ball was rolling once again. This time he would have yet another new ship—a steam-engined battering ram, named the *Roosevelt* after President Theodore Roosevelt, who was a great admirer and supporter of Peary's. Peary hoped that the *Roosevelt* would do what the *Windward* had failed to do: smash through the ice all the way to the edge of the Arctic Ocean itself, thus saving Peary hundreds of miles of debilitating sledge travel.

The Roosevelt *at Cape Sheridan, on the northern coast of Ellesmere Island. The ship was specially built to Peary's specifications to batter its way to the Arctic Ocean and withstand a long winter frozen in there.*

One of Peary's sledge parties battles its way through the ice toward a lead—*a watery break in the ice. The so-called Big Lead, which extended, according to Peary, "east and west across our course, farther than we could see," halted his northward progress for several days during both the 1906 and 1909 attempts at the Pole.*

If the *Roosevelt* succeeded in getting Peary close to the Arctic Ocean, Peary planned to institute his new brainchild, the so-called Peary system. He had decided to abandon his philosophy of traveling light with as few companions as possible. The Peary system would instead utilize three different squads of men; each squad would have many members, most of them Inuit. The first group would break a trail toward the Pole, building igloos along the way. The second party would follow behind the first on a rotational basis, carrying supplies forward and establishing permanent camps. The final party, including Peary, would move along this supply line, gradually overtaking the others until they were within striking distance of the Pole. At that point, Peary and a small party would shoot forward to the goal, after which they would follow their well-established supply line back to their point of origin.

On July 16, 1905, the *Roosevelt* steamed out of New York harbor under the command of the stout Newfound-

land sea captain Bob Bartlett. Captain Bartlett smashed his way up through the ice-clogged Kennedy and Robeson channels to Cape Sheridan, which lies on the tip of Ellesmere Island at the very edge of the great frozen ocean. There, the party made camp for the winter, and by February 1906, Peary was ready to test his system. Soon a moving, antlike relay line of 28 men along with 120 dogs was strung out northward across the ice, with Henson at the very front breaking trail. In acknowledgment of Henson's abilities, Peary told him, "To be damned sure we succeed, I'm sending you, Matt, out six days ahead of us with the pioneering party."

But the shifting, treacherous ice soon slowed the party to a crawl, and by March 25, after making just 70 miles, the line was stacked up at the edge of a black expanse of water that Peary named the Big Lead. The men were forced to wait a week before the lead froze over. Not long after they had all crossed over this thin, creaking ice field, they were struck by a blinding blizzard and had to hunker down in igloos to wait it out. Peary was in an agony of impatience and frustration. When the storm lifted, he measured his latitude and discovered that the drifting ice had carried his party almost 70 miles westward while it had been waiting for the weather to clear. He pushed furiously on ahead with a small party but soon found himself in a shifting network of drifting ice and open water. Still, though he and his men had begun killing and eating the dogs for food, he struggled northward. At a latitude that he calculated to be just above 87 degrees north, Peary "looked at the drawn faces of my comrades, at the skeleton figures of my few remaining dogs, at my nearly empty sledges, [and] I felt that I had cut the margin as narrow as could reasonably be expected." He called a halt to the march. As the others turned about and started the long journey back, Peary remained motionless for a long time, looking silently northward. He had set a new farthest north, but the Pole was still 300 miles away.

Ahab and Nemesis

Robert Peary turned 52 in May 1908. He had become by this time an Ahab-like figure, limping about on his mangled feet, his piercing but faraway gaze framed by his flowing gray beard and hair, sternly erect in posture but always leaning slightly forward as if he were pushing against some contrary polar wind or lashing a team of sled dogs before him, his thoughts always bent on the inscrutable and terrible white nemesis that had captivated him, crippled him, and eluded him. Many of his contemporaries thought he was cracked, monomaniacal, a deluded, obsessed old man. He was dead broke—having pumped every penny he owned into his Arctic exploration—physically and emotionally exhausted, in ill health, a veritable stranger to his friends and family. Dr. Frederick Cook called him a "weather-beaten fanatic . . . wrecked in physique, wrecked in ambition, wrecked in hope." And the object of his obsession, like Ahab's white whale, continued to defy him.

And yet, like Ahab, Peary would not yield. He still had influential supporters, the most important of whom was President Roosevelt, who perceived something distinctly and admirably American in Peary's struggle and who also felt that Peary had the best chance of planting the American flag at the top of the world. "I believe in you, Peary, and I believe in your success—if it is within the possibility of man," the president told him. And so, with the president's help, Peary once again secured the financial backing

President Theodore Roosevelt bids Peary farewell and good luck as the famed Arctic explorer prepares to set sail from Oyster Bay, Long Island, in June 1908 on what all agreed was sure to be—successful or not—his final polar voyage.

A few score of the 246 sled dogs Peary brought with him to the Arctic in 1908 doze or laze about the deck of the Roosevelt. *The greatest difference between the American (as well as the Norwegian) and the British methods of polar exploration was the British distrust of dogs as a method of transport.*

and the prerequisite leave from the navy he required to return to the hunt. In June 1908, with a crowd of onlookers cheering wildly—and with President Roosevelt himself standing on the dock shouting "Bully! Bully!"—the *Roosevelt* steamed out of the harbor at Oyster Bay, Long Island. Everyone, including the president, realized that this truly would be Peary's final assault on the North Pole, but not everyone agreed on the outcome. There were many in the crowd who believed that they had seen the last of Robert Peary.

Returning to the Arctic with Peary were Henson, Captain Bob Bartlett, and Ross Marvin, expedition secretary. Peary had also recruited the strapping Dr. John Goodsell as the expedition's physician; Donald MacMillan, a physical training instructor and Arctic enthusiast; and Yale

University athlete George Borup. The *Roosevelt* continued to take on supplies at various ports as it steamed northward, and when the ship left Etah, Greenland, for its final destination, it was carrying, among other things, a full load of coal, 70 tons of whale meat, the blubber of 50 walruses, 22 Inuit men with their hunting equipment, 17 Inuit women, 10 Inuit children, and 246 dogs. "To my dying day, I shall never forget the frightful noise, the choking stench, and the terrible confusion that reigned aboard," Captain Bartlett later wrote. This hectic ark pushed through the perilous ice of Kennedy and Robeson channels with the dogs yapping, the great ice floes grinding, and a sleepless Peary on deck gesturing and shouting at an equally sleepless Bartlett in the crow's nest.

Peary's private Arctic army arrived at Cape Sheridan on September 5. By late autumn, the entire army had moved 90 miles northwest to Cape Columbia. Located at the northern edge of Ellesmere Island, 475 miles away from the Pole, Cape Columbia would serve as Peary's jumping-off point, and it was quickly transformed into a bustling little town on the shores of the Arctic Ocean, the windows of its huts filled with hopeful light throughout the long Arctic night.

In early February 1909, with the temperature 50 degrees below zero, the first of Peary's divisions began moving northward, forming the initial links in the umbilical cord of men, dogs, igloos, and supply depots that he hoped to stretch to the Pole. Bartlett led the vanguard, breaking a trail with shovels and pickaxes through the jumble of ice. The other parties were soon strung out behind him, moving back and forth from the base camp as the line extended northward, pounding out a beaten path for Peary, who came last, slowly but steadily overtaking each successive party.

The trail breakers made good time initially, but by early March the going had become torturously slow. Huge pressure ridges, some of them the size of large buildings, were

thrown up by colliding ice floes, forcing Bartlett to make
exhausting and time-consuming detours. On March 5, as
the Polar night began to lift, the line was halted once again
by the Big Lead; they waited five days for it to freeze over
and then crept across the thin black ice as carefully as
thieves in a dark house.

   With the dim new light came a bitter, knife-sharp wind
from the east. It grew into a violent gale, tossing sledges
about and reducing visibility. The ice pack drifted this way
and that way, destroying the straight umbilical line Peary

Four hundred and seventy-five miles of "icy chaos" separated Cape Columbia from the North Pole. Among the most difficult obstacles to overcome were pressure ridges—craggy hillocks of ice, some the size of buildings, created by ice floes colliding with one another.

was depending on. The Inuits spoke nervously of the evil demons and spirits that haunted the ice, and some of them began turning back. Both the Inuits and the white men began to break under the strain. When expedition secretary Ross Marvin refused to let a sick Inuit boy ride back to base camp on his sled, the boy's cousin shot Marvin, disposed of his body in a hole in the ice, and traveled home on Marvin's sled, with his sick cousin riding comfortably along with him. (The Inuit reported simply that Marvin had fallen through the ice and drowned.) Far

Ooqueah, Ootah, Matthew Henson, Egingwah, and Seeglo celebrate having reached what they believed to be the North Pole.

ahead to the north, Peary, an ice demon in his own right, pushed on; he had passed all the parties except for the spearhead group, which now consisted of Henson, Bartlett, and several Inuit men. Peary drove them mercilessly before him.

On March 31, Bartlett and Henson reached 87 degrees north latitude—farther north than any human had ever been. Not long after, they were finally overtaken by Peary, who came up behind them on a sled pulled by 16 frenzied dogs. Now the entire umbilical was stretched out behind Peary, and he began making plans for the final break with his lifeline. The Pole was 150 miles ahead. Peary, his beard and mustache solidly frozen to his face, picked the men who would accompany him on the final dash—Henson and four Inuits, named Egingwah, Seeglo, Ootah, and Ooqueah. Bartlett, who had hoped desperately to go all the way to the Pole, wept bitterly as he turned back.

As the final two sledges shot forward, Peary could sense the nearness of his goal. He could taste it. After calling a halt early on the morning of April 6, 1909, Peary consulted his chronometer and took a measurement with his sextant. Then Peary watched his four Inuit companions and Henson build an igloo. When they had finished, Peary produced a small American flag and placed it atop the igloo. Henson, assuming that the raising of the flag indicated that the camp was of special significance, asked Peary about it. In reply, he was told that "this . . . is the last and most northerly camp on the earth" but not that Peary, after more than 20 years of Arctic exploration, had reached his goal. Later, Peary would write that the camp was just five miles from the Pole but that he was "actually too exhausted to realize at the moment that my life's purpose had been achieved" for all intents and purposes.

"The Pole at last!!!" he wrote in his diary after waking from a badly needed nap, then proceeded, by himself, to travel the last few miles. Later, during the return journey, he wrote, "My life work is accomplished. The thing which it was intended from the beginning that I should do, the thing which I believed could be done and that I could do, I have done. After 23 years of effort, hard work, disappointments, hardships, privations, more or less suffering, and some risks, I have won the last great geographical prize. My work is the finish, the cap and climax, of 300 years of effort, loss of life and expenditure of millions, by some of the best men of the civilized nations of the world, and it has been accomplished with a clean-cut dash, spirit, and, I believe, thoroughness characteristically American. I am content." Unfortunately, it seems that Peary had not reached the North Pole after all.

The first person to challenge Peary's claim was his old friend Dr. Cook. Peary was still on the *Roosevelt*, traveling homeward, when he was informed that Cook was claiming to have reached the Pole via Axel Heiberg Island in April 1908, well before Peary. Peary laughed aloud at the news; it was clearly preposterous. Cook had been in the Arctic and had been traveling with Inuits; he might even have reached the edge of the Arctic Ocean. But his claim to have marched across the ice to the Pole was outrageous. The following years would prove Peary to be correct on this matter; Cook was exposed as a fraud and a hoaxer. Humiliated, he was forced to flee the country in a silly disguise, and he lived out his remaining years in utter disgrace. Nevertheless, he had managed to steal—or at least to muffle—Peary's thunder, and during the feud with Peary that preceded Cook's ignominious exile, his supporters raised questions about the veracity of *Peary's* claim. And unlike the pathetic Cook, these questions would not go away.

Did Robert Peary reach the North Pole? The controversy over this question rages until this day; as recently as 1990, new evidence for and against Peary was being cited. The evidence against him has grown steadily over the years. His journal for the final days of the expedition was mysteriously—and in the opinion of many detractors, conveniently—edited in crucial places. Once he had "reached the Pole," Peary asked none of his companions to confirm his latitudinal measurements, and neither Henson nor the Inuit men were able to take their own measurements. His behavior on the return journey was characterized by his companions as morose, elusive, and even depressed; a strange way to act, especially for a man who has just achieved his life's goal. Moreover, he never stated directly to any of his companions at that time that he had reached the Pole. And, most tellingly, according to numerous experienced Arctic explorers, it is simply impossible for anyone—even as great an Arctic traveler as Peary—to have covered the distances he claimed to have traversed during his final five marches. Even if he did travel at the fantastic rate of speed he claimed, his assertion then relies on his having sledged, for those last five days, in an absolute straight line due north, with no adjustments necessary to account for the drift of the ice—a most unlikely scenario. But the most damning bit of evidence is that Peary simply

The New York Herald *of Tuesday, September 7, 1909, announces Peary's claim to have finally attained the "last great geographical prize."*

THE NEW YORK HERALD.

NEW YORK, TUESDAY, SEPTEMBER 7, 1909.—TWENTY-FOUR PAGES.— BY THE NEW YORK HERALD COMPANY.

ROBERT E. PEARY, AFTER 23 YEARS SIEGE, REACHES NORTH POLE; ADDS "THE BIG NAIL" TO NEW YORK YACHT CLUB'S TROPHIES; DR. COOK TO SUBMIT RECORDS TO UNIVERSITY OF DENMARK

could not offer any solid proof of his claim. Most of the explorers and analysts who have examined the evidence believe that at best, Peary came no closer than 60 miles to the Pole.

Peary has his supporters as well. They defend his reputation ferociously, asserting that the mileage Peary claimed for the final marches should be accepted simply because Peary was *Peary*, the greatest sledge-dog traveler in history. Confronted with the fact that in the end Peary offered only his word as proof, they say that Peary was an honorable man and that his word should be accepted. In the final analysis, however, the burden of proof in such cases clearly and rightfully lies with the explorer.

Did Peary lie? Perhaps he did; perhaps he lied to himself. If he did, it was because he had placed too great a burden on himself, a burden of dreams that in the end proved too heavy for even a man of his strength to carry. Ironically, his achievements, even if he did indeed fall short of the Pole, rank him with the greatest of explorers. But for Peary, anything less than the Pole was failure. Perhaps, after that final march, realizing that the Pole was still too far away and that he could not reach it and return alive, Peary simply succumbed to the unfairness of it all and decided that he was close enough and that he deserved this victory. If these were his thoughts and feelings at that moment, he was justified in one sense—Robert Peary, of all men, deserved to be remembered as the conqueror of the North Pole.

Robert Peary died on February 20, 1920, taking with him to his grave whatever secrets he still harbored. Unless new evidence is unearthed, he will not be remembered as the undisputed conqueror of the North Pole—whether he in truth reached it or whether he did not—and so his nemesis eludes him still. If restless spirits do haunt the frozen, desolate reaches of the Arctic, as the Inuit believe, Peary's is certainly among them.

Further Reading

Berton, Pierre. *The Arctic Grail: The Quest for the Northwest Passage and the North Pole, 1818–1909.* New York: Viking, 1988.

Davies, Thomas D. "New Evidence Places Peary at Pole." *National Geographic*, Jan. 1990, 44–60.

Dodge, Ernest S. *The Polar Rosses: John and James Clark Ross and Their Explorations.* New York: HarperCollins, 1973.

Dolan, Edward F. *Matthew Henson, Black Explorer.* New York: Dodd, Mead, 1979.

Gilman, Michael. *Matthew Henson.* New York: Chelsea House, 1988.

Hall, Sam. *The Fourth World.* New York: Knopf, 1987.

Herbert, Wally. "Did He Reach the Pole?" *National Geographic*, Sept. 1988, 387–413.

————. *The Noose of Laurels: Robert E. Peary and the Race to the North Pole.* New York: Atheneum, 1989.

Hunt, William R. *To Stand at the Pole: The Dr. Cook-Admiral Peary Controversy.* New York: Stein & Day, 1981.

Kirwan, L.P. *A History of Polar Exploration.* New York: Norton, 1960.

Miller, Floyd. *Ahdoolo: The Biography of Matthew A. Henson.* New York: Dutton, 1963.

Mirsky, Jeannette. *To the Arctic: The Story of Northern Exploration from Earliest Times to the Present.* New York: Knopf, 1948.

Neatby, Leslie. *Conquest of the Last Frontier.* Athens: Ohio University Press, 1966.

Parry, Ann. *Parry of the Arctic: The Life Story of Admiral Sir Edward Parry.* London: Chatto & Windus, 1963.

Rawlins, Dennis. *Peary at the North Pole: Fact or Fiction?* Washington, DC: Robert B. Luce, 1973.

Weems, John Edward. *Peary: The Explorer and the Man.* Boston: Houghton Mifflin, 1967.

Wright, Theon. *The Big Nail: The Story of the Cook-Peary Feud.* New York: John Day, 1970.

Chronology

Entries in roman refer directly to Robert Peary and the exploration of the North Pole; entries in Italic refer to important historical and cultural events of the era.

c. 320 B.C.E. *The Greek explorer Pthaeas sails from the southern coast of modern-day France around Great Britain to an island now thought to be Iceland*

c. 700–800 *Irish monks establish settlements on the Orkney, Shetland, and Faroe islands, and also in Iceland*

c. 870 *Norwegian Vikings colonize the Icelandic countryside*

c. 985 *Eric the Red settles in present-day Greenland*

mid 1200's-mid 1500's *Norway declines as a naval power and abandons Arctic settlements; English and Scottish merchants begin whale hunting in the Arctic region*

1607 *British explorer Henry Hudson, in search of a water route connecting the Atlantic and Pacific Oceans, attempts to reach this passage by sailing over the top of the globe through the North Pole*

1616 *English navigator William Baffin discovers a bay along the coast of Greenland that today bears his name*

1775 *British naval captain James Cook discovers the continent of Antarctica*

late 1700s–1800s *Numerous British, American, and Scandinavian adventurers and scientists attempt to reach the North Pole; although none are successful in reaching the Pole, they gather important geographical, navigational, and scientific data along the way*

May 6, 1856 Robert Edwin Peary born in Cresson, Pennsylvania.

1860 *American explorer Isaac Hayes discovers that, contrary to long-held popular belief, the Arctic sea is frozen; Many explorers try to sledge across the frozen sea, but none reach the Pole*

1885	While working as an engineer, Peary travels to Nicaragua to survey the site for a proposed canal linking the Atlantic and Pacific Oceans, which is later built in Panama
1886	Gains publicity after exploring the uncharted interior of Greenland
1887	Becomes field leader of canal survey project in Nicaragua; marries Josephine Diebitsch on August 11; Matthew Henson becomes Peary's assistant
1891–1895	Peary makes numerous expeditions to the Arctic region, meeting with the Inuit and crossing the polar ice cap; in 1893, Fridtjof Nansen attempts to reach the North Pole but is unsuccessful
1898	Peary makes his first attempt to reach the North Pole by sailing up Smith Sound to Greenland or Ellesmere Island and then marching north over the frozen ice; the plan does not succeed
1905	With the support of President Roosevelt, Peary makes another attempt to reach the North Pole, using the Peary system of creating a supply line along the route; he fails to reach his goal, but sets a new farthest north
1908	Obsessed with being the first to reach the North Pole, he embarks on another Arctic expedition
1909	Returns home claiming to have reached the North Pole on April 6 with Henson and four Inuit; American Frederick Cook claims to have reached the Pole in 1908, but is later disproven
Feb. 20, 1920	Peary dies in Washington, D.C.
1990	After many decades of debate, the Navigation Foundation determines that Peary did reach within five miles of the North Pole

Index

Picture Credits

The Bettmann Archive: pp. 12, 43, 51; Biblioteque Nationale, Paris: cover (map); Bowdoin College Library, Special Collections: p. 26; Center for Polar Archives, The National Archives: pp. 39, 40; Library of Congress: p. 88 (neg. # LC-USZ62-42993); New Bedford Whaling Museum: pp. 62–63; New York Public Library, Astor, Lenox and Tilden Foundations, General Research Division: pp. 46, 48–49 Adolphus Washington Greeley, *Three Years of Arctic Service*. Scribner's Sons (New York) 1886; 35, 37 Charles Francis Hall, *Arctic Researches and Life Among the Esquimaux*. Harper & Bros. (New York) 1865; 29, 32 33, 34 Elisha Kent Kane, *Arctic Explorations: The Second Grinnell Expedition in Search of Sir John Franklin*. Childs & Peterson (Philadelphia) 1856; 72 Fridtjof Nansen, *Farthest North*. Harper & Bros. (New York) 1897; 24–25 W. E. Parry, *Journal of a Voyage for Discovery of a North West Passage in 1819–20, in His Majesty's Ships, Hecla & Gripper*. J. Murray (London) 1828; 18–19 W. E. Parry. *Narrative of an Attempt to Reach the North Pole in Boats Attached to His Majesty's Ship Hecla in 1827*. J. Murray (London) 1828; 60 (bottom), 64 Sir John Ross, *Narrative of a Second Voyage in Search of a Northwest Passage*. A.W. Webster (London) 1835; 60–61 (top) Sir John Ross *A Voyage of Discovery Made Under Orders of the Admiralty in His Majesty's Ships, Isabella & Alexander for the Purpose of Exploring Baffin's Bay*. Hurst, Rees, Orme and Brown (London) 1819; 22, 38 George E. Tyson. *Arctic Experiences*. Harper & Bros. (New York) 1894; New York Public Library, Astor, Lenox and Tilden Foundations, Rare Book and Manuscript Division: pp. 58 (top and bottom), 59 (top and bottom); Peabody Museum of Salem: p. 57; From *Peary*, by William Herbert Hobbs, MacMillan (New York) 1936: pp. 28, 44; Peary-MacMillan Arctic Museum, Bowdoin College. p. 94; Admiral Robert E. Peary c National Geographic Society: cover (portrait), pp. 15, 52, 54–55, 66, 67, 69, 70, 71, 77, 84, 89, 91, 92, 96, 98–99, 100; Universitetsbiblioteket, Oslo: pp. 14, 78, 80, 81, 82; Weidenfeld and Nicholson, Ltd., London: p. 61

Christopher Dwyer has written many books on historical subjects for young adult readers. He lives in Philadelphia, Pennsylvania.

William H. Goetzmann holds the Jack S. Blanton, Sr., Chair in History at the University of Texas at Austin, where he has taught for many years. The author of numerous works on American history and exploration, he won the 1967 Pulitzer and Parkman prizes for his *Exploration and Empire: The Role of the Explorer and Scientist in the Winning of the American West, 1800–1900*. With his son William N. Goetzmann, he coauthored *The West of the Imagination*, which received the Carr P. Collins Award in 1986 from the Texas Institute of Letters. His documentary television series of the same name received a blue ribbon in the history category at the American Film and Video Festival held in New York City in 1987. A recent work, *New Lands, New Men: America and the Second Great Age of Discovery*, was published in 1986 to much critical acclaim.

Michael Collins served as command module pilot on the *Apollo 11* space mission, which landed his colleagues Neil Armstrong and Buzz Aldrin on the moon. A graduate of the United States Military Academy, Collins was named an astronaut in 1963. In 1966 he piloted the *Gemini 10* mission, during which he became the third American to walk in space. The author of several books on space exploration, Collins was director of the Smithsonian Institution's National Air and Space Museum from 1971 to 1978 and is a recipient of the Presidential Medal of Freedom.